Excuse Me, College Is Now

Also by Doreen Banaszak

Excuse Me, Your Life Is Now

EXCUSE ME,
College Is Now

How to Be a Success
in School and in Life

Doreen Banaszak and Sebastian Oddo

HAMPTON ROADS
PUBLISHING COMPANY, INC.

Cover design by Jane Hagaman
Cover: Goldfish ©American Images, Inc./Getty Images;
Water ©iStockphoto.com

Hampton Roads Publishing Company, Inc.
1125 Stoney Ridge Road
Charlottesville, VA 22902

434-296-2772
fax: 434-296-5096
e-mail: hrpc@hrpub.com
www.hrpub.com

If you are unable to order this book from your local
bookseller, you may order directly from the publisher.
Call 1-800-766-8009, toll-free.

Library of Congress Cataloging-in-Publication Data

Banaszak, Doreen, 1965-
Excuse me, college is now : how to be a success in school and in life /
Doreen Banaszak and Sebastian Oddo.
    p. cm.
Includes index.
Summary: "Drawing upon the principles of the Law of Attraction, this
book
provides students with the opportunity to create the college experience
they
truly desire"--Provided by publisher.
    ISBN 978-1-57174-592-7 (5.5 x 8.5 tp : alk. paper)
    1. College student orientation. 2. College students--Conduct of life. I.
Oddo, Sebastian, 1985- II. Title.
    LB2343.3.B36 2009
    378.1'98--dc22
                                        2008054435

ISBN 978-1-57174-592-7
10 9 8 7 6 5 4 3 2 1
Printed on acid-free paper in the United States

Doreen:
To Sammi, my best creation ever

Sebastian:
To Bandy, thank you for being there for Mom

Contents

Acknowledgments

would like to thank the usual suspects: Amy, for support; Zyon, Hannah, Jordan, for love; and Sammi, for making me laugh when I needed it most. Thank you to everyone at Hampton Roads, especially Jack for his vision and Jessica for her amazing editing skills.

Finally to Sebastian, for his desire to help his fellow students. I'm glad you got in touch with me when the concept for this book came to you!

Doreen Banaszak

am so happy and grateful that I have the opportunity to write a book. I have attracted some wonderful people that must be thanked before I begin. First and foremost, I would like to thank my coauthor, Doreen Banaszak, for all her guidance and support. If it weren't for you believing in my story and my purpose in life, I am not sure where my idea about this book would have gone. Jack Jennings, thank you for taking the risk and accepting my proposal. Special thanks to Jessica Swope for your editing contribution. Your hard work added huge value to the final product!

To all of my teachers over the years who knew there was something special about me, who connected with me and took extra time to help me when I needed someone there: I respect all of you for what you do each and every day—*thank you*. To the authors of the books that helped me overcome my anxiety: Lynn Grabhorn, my guardian angel, is the reason why there is an "Excuse Me" series and why this book now exists. The night after I finished her book *Excuse Me, Your Life Is Waiting*, I e-mailed her, and the following morning I received an e-mail back. Now that's real dedication! For the rest of my life, I will follow and teach her practices to everyone and anyone who is willing to listen. Karen Salmansohn, Cesar Millan, Judith Orloff, Rhonda Byrne, the Dalai Lama, Bradley Trevor Greive, and Dr. Wayne Dyer are just a few of the many authors who have inspired me to help others, write this book, be positive, and look forward to an exciting future!

Each one of my friends holds a special place in my heart. They all possess different qualities and characteristics that I admire. It's like having your choice of different chocolates to eat—if you had the same milk chocolate each time around, life would be boring. To my loving family, thank you for understanding my mission with PFR (PositiveFeelingsRule.com) and thank you for spreading the word to everyone you know and have come across in life.

John, the way you communicate with others has inspired me to follow in your footsteps and always strive to better communicate with people. You have taught me many lessons that I plan to discuss in this book and share with others. Tina, my little sister, your strength has inspired me to do more in life. With every new stage in your life, you always seem to handle it with great strength. In fact, I think you have one of the best solutions for when you are feeling down—you party! I love you for teaching me that.

Mom, your positive attitude was very contagious from an early age. I watched how you turned negative circumstances in your life into positive ones. You never let anything or anyone control you. You were always the captain of your ship. One of the greatest examples of this is how you completely healed yourself of multiple sclerosis (MS). Thank you for never putting any restraints on what I wanted to do in life. I love you.

Dad, if it weren't for you finding that Lynn Grabhorn book I am not sure where my life would have gone. You were there for me when I was going through some of the roughest times in my life and would not stop helping me until I felt better. You have been my personal life coach and health counselor and I love you for that.

Buster Brown, my baby Shih Tzu, I know you are a dog but you have taught me a great lesson in life: never hold grudges. You are never mad at me, no matter what I do to you. You make me so happy, and I love you for that.

Last, and most importantly, my fiancée and soon to be wife

Charly-Ann—you are what keeps me powered during the day, and what I look forward to coming home to at night. You are the reason I made it through college, the one who stood by my side when I was depressed, and the one who consistently told me I didn't have a learning disability. Because of you, I look forward to the future. I am so grateful for everything you have helped me with in my life. I am also so proud of all the amazing things you have done on your own. You have taught me a very valuable tool, which is simply how to *relax*. This has helped me so much! I am so excited for our future and I know we are going to leave many positive footprints on this earth! I love you so much.

Sebastian Oddo

Introduction

"I'm so afraid I'm going to fail."
"My class load is too much this semester."
"I miss home."
"I wish I had more friends."
"I never have enough time."
"I thought college was supposed to be the 'best time of my life.'"

Not too long ago when I was in college, I heard many people making comments such as these and, to be honest, I heard myself expressing many of the same sentiments (when I wasn't saying them out loud, I was certainly feeling them). It seemed that no matter how much fun we were having, that "fun" was always undermined by the fears, doubts, worries, and anxieties that we were all struggling with on some level.

Any of this sound familiar?

Think about it: You are thrown into a whole new world with a whole new set of expectations and responsibilities. You not only have to deal with new academic demands that are far more rigorous than those of high school, but you are now required to make decisions and do things you've never had to do before. You are suddenly anonymous and have to learn how to navigate your way around a world that barely resembles the safe, comfortable world you left behind. And on top of that, you have to do this all by yourself, away from the support system you have known all your life.

The truth is, your college years are going to be among the most challenging and memorable times of your life. Your experience can be filled with excitement, fun, happiness, and growth, *or* it can be tainted by fear, anxiety, frustration, and confusion. Through what I thought was a stroke of luck, I soon became aware that I did indeed have a choice over the experience I was going to have, and when I was willing to make the conscious choice, my whole college experience changed.

Going into college, I had read lots of "college survival" books, but no matter what practical things I learned or tried to apply to my life, I just couldn't shake the undercurrent of fear that seemed to be holding me back from really embracing my college experience. On top of all the social and personal disappointments that were adding up, academically speaking, things were not going well—I wasn't getting the grades I wanted or that my family expected of me. My father suggested I read a book by Lynn Grabhorn called *Excuse Me, Your Life Is Waiting*, which was about the Law of Attraction and how to use it to *create* your life, rather than be a victim to it or passive observer of it. Until I read this book, I had never even considered that I could create the life I had always wanted for myself. Prior to this, I had always thought that what I had to do was what was expected of me or to react appropriately to any given situation.

I had no idea that this Law of Attraction was becoming so popular. I started hearing a lot about it and discovered that a lot of adults were using it to recreate their lives. They were using it to create more wealth, change careers, find their soul mates, and experience more fulfillment in their daily lives. I started to think that if this law could be used to create all of that, then it must also be able to create the grades, classes, roommate, professors, and overall college experience I wanted.

I started applying the principles I learned from the book to my college experience, and it wasn't long before college became a completely different world. I had more time to get my work done; papers were easier to write and presentations became fun, not stressful; I started getting the grades I wanted; my relationships with my roommate, neighbors, and professors all improved; and I started to realize how supportive my friends and family really were. Best of all, I was able to have more *fun*. That undercurrent of fear? Completely gone! College became what I had wanted it to be: fun, exciting, and challenging (in a good, rather than oppressive way). Using the principles of the Law of Attraction, college shaped up to be "the best time of my life." This is what I want for you, too!

After college, I was fortunate enough to team up with Doreen Banaszak, author of *Excuse Me, Your Life Is Now*, the follow-up to Lynn's book. In her book, Doreen addresses how to overcome obstacles in applying the Law of Attraction. Together we have written this book to give you the formula to create the college experience you want, not the one you think you "have to" have. We will teach you how to apply the formula directly to your college experience so that you can create the emotional, academic, physical, and social results you *really* want.

You may feel some resistance to the idea of adding more reading to your seemingly endless list of reading assignments. Completely understandable. But if you're willing to consider that you could actually thrive in college, and not just survive college, then this book will be well worth your time, because it shows how to do just that.

So are you ready to make the choice to create your college experience, rather than be a victim of it? Then read on and Doreen and I will show you how.

Chapter 1

CREATING YOUR LIFE 101

I know of no more encouraging fact than the unquestioned ability of a man to elevate his life by conscious endeavor.

—Henry David Thoreau

Before we get started, I want to acknowledge that everything I'm about to share with you in this book is going to sound pretty different from what you've learned so far about how it is that you get what you want in this life. Up until this point, you have probably heard things like:

"No pain, no gain."

"Success is earned, not given."

"You are what you are; make the best of it."

"Work on your weaknesses."

What these expressions get at is a value that is pervasive in our society, which is that life is meant to be difficult; that to be successful and have a happy life, we must always be on our A-game; that only the strong survive; and that only the most ruthlessly ambitious and self-disciplined can thrive.

Imagine going through not just the next four years, but the next twenty years with this kind of mentality. Then one day, if you are lucky, you experience a midlife crisis that forces you to consider that there is another way entirely to go about living your life. As I mentioned in the introduction, a lot of adults have hit this wall and have been turned on to the Law of Attraction. Slowly but surely, inspired by a midlife crisis that changes their perspective, they learn that the old beliefs they've lived by are not as fixed (or even as true) as they had always believed them to be; their life does not "have to" be anything, it can actually be whatever they want it to be.

I will be the first to admit that I fell for all those "truisms" about success—all of them! I truly believed them, and lived them, and my experience became just what they promised: my life was hard and the most I could hope for was that it wouldn't get any harder. I am so grateful that I didn't have to wait for a midlife crisis to wise up. I'm hoping to catch you early enough so that, like me, you can learn the truth that I was fortunate enough to stumble upon: you can have all that you want *right now*. I invite you to open up your mind to some new concepts and, more important, actually try them out and see if they resonate as truth with you. You'll know truth when you feel it—it's that sense you get when you just know you are right, no matter what anybody else says or thinks.

WHAT IS THE LAW OF ATTRACTION?

So, what is the Law of Attraction and how can your conscious use of it create the college experience you really want? Scientifically speaking, it has been identified that everything is made up of energy and that all energy comes together and pulls apart to become the reality we observe. As humans, we give off energy in the form of feelings, thoughts, words, and actions. Some of that energy can be considered positive energy, that is, happy feelings, upbeat thoughts, pleasant words, and thoughtful actions. Other energy can be considered negative energy, that is, angry feelings, destructive thoughts, spiteful words, and selfish actions. What science is proving is that the energy we give off actually attracts and creates all of our external reality, *all* of it. Think about it for a second: What happens to your reality when you die? Does it exist if you're not there to observe it? How could it?! If we look at it this way, then you have to be the creator of your reality.

For all you non–science majors out there, this is what it all comes down to: *like attracts like*. If, for example, you are sending out positive, success-oriented energy into the world—feelings of success, thoughts of success, words of success, actions that reflect success—then you will ultimately attract opportunities to experience more success in your reality. Seems simple enough, right? Then why aren't you consciously using this approach all the time to create the experiences you want? The answer to this question is slightly more complex.

Most of us are conditioned to believe that something "out there," whatever it is, will make us happy. Our time is spent saying things like, "I'll be happy when I get into the college I want," or "I'll be happy when I ace the exam," or "I'll be happy when so-and-so likes me," and so on. What typically happens when we "get" all those things? We start saying things like, "I'll be happy when I get the job I want, when I finish this project, when so-and-so marries me." What happens to happiness in all of this? It may be experienced for a little while, but the feeling is ultimately fleeting. Why? Because we've attached happiness to some thing/person/event in our external reality. If you haven't noticed by now, reality changes (a lot!), and because of this, once we get the "thing" that will bring us happiness, we start to fear that if that "thing" goes away, then we won't be happy, or we decide that there has to be more happiness, so we go off to create the next big thing that will bring us the happiness we desire. This creates a perpetual cycle in which we are always striving for happiness, and more happiness, and more happiness. We're so busy chasing happiness that those times when we actually do experience happiness are few and far between.

Let me ask you a very important question: Where does your experience of happiness exist? Where does happiness exist? Is it something that exists outside you, attributable to something or someone "out there"? Or is it something that you experience from within? The answer may seem obvious, but it's worth looking at. Happiness exists inside you and is experienced from within. If happiness exists inside of you, me, and everybody else, then it is an experience, not a thing. Doesn't it seem just a little bit crazy to say then that we need something *outside of us* in order to experience something we have *inside of us* right now, 24/7? You bet it does, and it's the reason why so many of us are chasing happiness, joy, wealth, abundance, and success, instead of experiencing all of those things right now.

Let's get back to what actually causes happiness. Well, what *is* happiness? It is an essence, an invisible concept, a state of being that we describe as a physical experience. It is something we feel. To feel something, it has to exist before we feel it or else we couldn't feel it. That means that the state of being of happiness, the invisible concept, has to exist and therefore precede the feeling of happiness. Ever have one of those moments when you just feel happy and you don't even know why, you just are? That's how you know the state of being of happiness had to precede the feeling because you weren't consciously thinking, "I'm going to feel happy now" or "That song made me happy"; you just physically experienced it. This is important because we tend to identify with what we are feeling and not what is causing the feeling, a state of being. Bear with me here.

Happiness (an invisible state of being) becomes a physical experience through feelings, thoughts, words, actions, and our perception of physical reality. So state of being is the cause of our feelings, thoughts, words, actions, and perception of physical reality. (At this point, you must feel like you unknowingly picked up a philosophy book. Don't worry! We will shortly get to the practical applications of all of this, particularly in regard to your college experience.) If state of being is *cause*, then our feelings, thoughts, words, actions, and perception of physical reality are *effects* of the state of being we are currently experiencing. It turns out that all this time we've been focusing on the effects of our state of being instead of looking at our state of being as the actual cause of the effect. If we want happiness as our effect, for example, then our attention needs to be on experiencing the state of being of happiness right now.

WHAT CREATES AND WHAT ARE YOU CREATING?

Some self-help experts suggest that your thoughts create; just *think* positively, they say, and you'll be all set. Or they say things like your feelings create, so just *be* happy, or that your words create, so just *say* you're happy, or that your actions create, so just *act* positively. Or even more broadly, they say that *all* these things create, so be sure you are *watching and acting on all of them all the time* and you'll be good to go. What they say is fine, but it's exhausting just thinking about it, isn't it? It just doesn't make sense that something we are already doing unconsciously—creating—would be so complex when we do it consciously.

If feelings, thoughts, words, and actions are all *effects* of the state of being you are experiencing, it makes sense that to create what you want, you need only keep your attention on your current state of being. When you do, the energy you send out through your feelings, thoughts, words, and actions will reflect and expand your current state of being. What we are actually constantly creating are opportunities to experience more of our current state of being. Let me repeat: *You are always creating opportunities to experience more of your current state of being.*

You are not creating failing grades, you are not creating an inconsiderate roommate, you are not creating the zero balance in your checking account, and you are not creating the fact that your parents disapprove of your behavior. What you are creating are opportunities to experience more of your current state of being of failure, frustration, lack, judgment, or whatever other feelings those events evoke for you.

Let's take a look at some basic, fundamental states of being:

- Happiness / Sadness
- Freedom / Fear
- Peace / Panic
- Abundance / Limitation
- Love / Hate
- Success / Failure
- Fulfillment / Need
- Wealth / Lack
- Connectedness / Loneliness
- Confidence / Insecurity
- Clarity / Confusion
- Stability / Depression
- Security / Jealousy
- Calm / Anxiety

Notice how each is the opposite of the other in these pairs. If you pause to consider your own experience, you'll find that it is impossible to experience one at the exact time you're experiencing its opposite. Think of them as two sides of the same coin. You are experiencing one or the other in any given moment—never both.

Let's simplify this: if there were two worlds, the world of acceptance and the world of resistance, then all the "positive" states of being would exist in the world of acceptance and all the "negative" states of being would exist in the world of resistance. So, when you come right down to it, you are either experiencing acceptance or resistance.

At this point you may be thinking, "Well, it seems that all I have to do is put my attention on experiencing the states of being that reflect acceptance and I'll be just fine." This would seem to make sense, but let's take a closer look at that strategy. What if I said: "I want you right now to *not* picture a pink elephant in your mind. Really, just don't picture a pink elephant." What are you thinking about and picturing right now? My bet would be a pink elephant. Why? Because I asked you *not* to. I asked you to resist picturing a pink elephant. Now what happened? You were experiencing a state of being of resistance and it expanded into your thoughts by picturing exactly what I asked you not to picture—a pink elephant.

You may be familiar with the phrase "What you resist persists." When you resist a state of being, all your attention becomes focused on it, making it impossible to experience its opposite. So the best strategy is just not to resist any state of being. If we practice acceptance of our current state of being instead of resisting it, when a less than desirable state of being arises (like anger or fear), all we can do is simply accept that we are experiencing it. The actual definition of acceptance is "to be open and receiving." When we are accepting, we are no longer resisting and therefore no longer *expanding* the experience of resistance, so we become open and receptive to the opposite state of being. If you were to accept everything, I mean *everything*, you would be truly free. The only reason anything has power over us is because we say it is not okay or we don't want to experience it. We become trapped by our resistance to that thing or experience. We become free when we are willing to say, "I'm experiencing it and it doesn't matter. It's okay." For example, if you say that you are experiencing fear and it doesn't matter, how can fear have any power over you? It can't! Acceptance equals freedom. Isn't that what we really want to experience?

Your greatest opportunity now is to realize that happiness, success, wealth, freedom, joy, and abundance all exist inside of you right now and become a physical reality through the energy of your feelings, thoughts, words, and actions. When you accept your current state of being, you are open and receptive to more physical experiences that expand the state of being of acceptance which includes all the "positive" states of being you really want to experience. Your willingness to experience these *now* will become your power to create opportunities to experience more of them in your life. This is the power available to you *right now*; this is the Law of Attraction!

WHAT IS YOUR ROLE IN ALL OF THIS?

Quantum physics has shown that reality, far from being definite, is actually pretty malleable. Scientists are proving that, in a very real way, we have the power to create our own reality. The states of being we've discussed expand and create opportunities to form and change your physical reality. Sounds good at first, but that can make some of us nervous. I mean, who among us wants to take responsibility for creating war, crime, a failing economy, or, perhaps a more immediate concern, failing out of college? Remember, it's not that you are creating those things, it's that you are *creating opportunities to experience more of the states of being those things are reflecting.*

It's important at this point to be willing to consider that you are the creator of your reality. If you can get that far, then you have gotten over the hurdle that most people never quite overcome, which is the belief that we are mere victims, passive to the forces of reality over which we have no control. Because it's impossible to be a creator and a victim at the same time, to be a creator, you have to be a creator *absolutely*. This means that you are completely free to create, that you cannot be hindered by anything, including the reality you've already created. Talk about power!

I'm going to ask you to consider one more thing: you are not alone in your ability to create. Believe it or not, you have a creation partner that helps you out in all of this. The job of your creation partner is to figure out the "how" of how something comes into your physical experience. Think about a thousand-piece jigsaw puzzle. You have all the pieces lying in front of you and, in your hand, you hold a specific piece, but you've lost the lid of the box and don't have any sense of what the final product is going to look like, or where the piece you hold is supposed to fit in the larger context of the puzzle. In this scenario, your piece represents your experience, and all the other pieces are things that make up all the possibilities that you can't envision. Your creation partner sees the picture on the box, so to speak, and sees how the pieces all fit together to give you what you want. In this way, your creation partner helps you to orchestrate into your experience what you truly desire, in a way that works in the context of the big picture of your life. Some call this partner "Universe" or "God" or "Genie." It doesn't matter what name you use. What matters is that your creation partner is there to deliver all that you say you want to experience in the physical world.

Ever had one of those experiences when you think about someone and later in the day bump into them? Or when you want something that seems impossible to get and somehow it just shows up? That's your creation partner aligning the physical world to deliver opportunities to experience more of your current state of being.

Your job is to communicate with your creation partner through your state of being. If you are experiencing lack and fear, your creation partner can only create more physical opportunities to experience lack and fear. If you are experiencing happiness and success, then your creation partner can create more physical opportunities for you to experience happiness and success.

That said, don't just "fake it until you make it." As you were reading the preceding, you may have had some of these thoughts: "But I really don't feel happy," or "I really think this exam is going to be hard," or "I really don't believe I am going to get the class I want." Let's be clear here—I am not asking you to pretend that you are experiencing something you're not. I'm inviting you to be aware of the state of being you are experiencing so that you can grow to be accepting of each state. Once you accept it, then you are open to experiencing the state of being you want. It is the difference between saying "I am happy" when you are actually experiencing sadness versus "I accept that I'm experiencing sadness right now, and that's okay." If you are pretending to experience a state of being, you are actually experiencing resistance, plain and simple. Contrary to your best intentions, that is what you end up expanding!

LET'S REVIEW

The Law of Attraction, like attracts like, is a universal law and is the explanation for what exists in our reality.

State of being is cause—it becomes physical through our feelings, thoughts, words, actions, and physical reality.

You are always creating opportunities to experience more of your current state of being; therefore you are always attracting opportunities in your physical reality to experience more of your current state of being.

Acceptance is your key to experiencing more of the states of being you want to experience.

You communicate with your creation partner through your current state of being, and your partner delivers physical opportunities to experience more of your current state of being.

You are a creator, not a victim of your experience!

Okay, so what do you do next? Two things:

1. Become and stay aware of your current state of being.

2. Accept whatever state of being you are experiencing.

STAYING AWARE AND ACCEPTING YOUR CURRENT STATE OF BEING

Since state of being is cause, the easiest way to keep tabs on your state of being is to consider your feelings, thoughts, words, and actions as reflections of your current state of being. Use them as tools to point you back to your current state of being so that you can practice accepting it, whatever it happens to be in the present moment. Pay attention to how you are feeling, what you are thinking, what you are saying, and what you are doing. It may seem like a lot to be aware of, but if you are willing to try the following exercise, you will see that it is actually easier than trying to keep your eye on everything that is happening around you in your external reality.

FEELINGS

Declare the following out loud and pay attention to any physical reactions you might have in your body:

I am resistance.

What did your body do? Did you experience tension? Did your stomach constrict? Did your jaw tighten? Did you feel the weight of the world on your shoulders? Did your throat constrict? These are some of the physical feelings people describe when the state of being of resistance becomes physical in the form of feelings. What happened for you? When you feel this way, you know that you are experiencing resistance.

A great example of this experience is when you are studying for a test, engrossed and happy in your progress, when your friend walks up and tells you that the exam was really hard and that half the morning session of the same class failed the exam. You probably experience a tightening of your muscles, a temperature change, and a sinking sensation in your stomach. These feelings are all reflections of a state of being of resistance, whether you describe that state as fear, stress, anxiety, panic, doubt, or worry.

Okay, now declare the following out loud and pay attention to what happens physically in your body:

I am acceptance.

Did you feel a relief? How about a little bit of a buzz in your stomach? Did you feel a smile come across your face? Did you feel your body expand out? Did you feel a weight lift off your shoulders? What happened for you? When you are feeling these things, you know that you are experiencing a state of being of acceptance, which can include happiness, joy, abundance, peace, fulfillment, and so on.

Once you are aware of what state of being your feelings reflect, you want to accept that state of being so that you expand opportunities to experience more acceptance. Here's what I invite you to say to yourself:

"I accept that I'm experiencing [insert state of being] right now, and that's okay."

Let's go back to the studying example. Your friend delivers the news, you feel your body tighten, you know you are experiencing fear, so instead of denying or resisting what's happening to you because it's unpleasant, simply say to yourself, "I accept that I'm experiencing fear right now, and that's okay."

If we aren't aware of the state of being we are experiencing and therefore don't accept it, what happens? We expand opportunities to experience more of that very state of being. If, for example, we watch the news and hear something frightening (which isn't a stretch given the kinds of stories that make it to the evening news) and experience the state of being of fear but immediately shut it out, we will find ourselves experiencing more fear and resistance throughout our day. It is not until we become aware and accepting that we can actually create in a new direction.

So, be aware of what you are feeling and get into the habit of asking yourself what state of being your feelings reflect and, no matter what answer you come up with, accept whatever state of being it is!

THOUGHTS AND WORDS

Pay attention to your thoughts. You'll notice that it doesn't take much for them to spiral out of control. How easy is it for us to go from "I need more time to write this paper" to "I'm never going to finish this paper" to "If I don't finish this paper, I'm going to fail" to "If I fail, my parents are going to kill me," and on and on. They don't call it a "train of thought" for nothing. It's like we get on the train and no matter how many times we pull the cord to signal our stop, the train just keeps going—full speed ahead!

We can't get off a train we are not even aware we are on, so the first step, then, is to become aware. But how do we do this? Be willing to listen to what we are thinking! Let's go back to the previous example, to the thought that started the whole train going: "I need more time to write this paper." As soon as you hear the word "need" in your head, you are saying that you don't have what you want. How can a creator not have what they want, when they can simply create it? The thought that you "need" anything becomes your opportunity to actually get off the train. When you hear it, simply recognize that you are experiencing a state of being of need and accept it. "I accept that I'm experiencing need right now, and that's okay."

Always ask yourself what states of being your thoughts are reflecting. Here are a few examples of some thoughts and how to accept the state of being they are reflecting:

"There is too much competition to get into the college I want."—"I accept that I'm experiencing limitation right now, and that's okay."

"Midterm exams are a killer."—"I accept that I'm experiencing fear right now, and that's okay."

"That class will fill before I get online to register for it."—"I accept that I'm experiencing lack right now, and that's okay."

"I'm never going to finish this term paper."—"I accept that I'm experiencing anxiety right now, and that's okay."

The same process is true with your words. Sometime try listening to everything you say just for an hour. You'll be amazed at all the resistant things that come not only into your mind, but also out of your mouth. Trust me, we all seem to be on the same train. Here are some particular words that can clue you into the state of being of resistance and how to accept it:

"I need . . ."—"I accept that I'm experiencing need right now, and that's okay."

"I can't . . ."—"I accept that I'm experiencing limitation right now, and that's okay."

"It's not possible for me to . . ."—"I accept that I'm experiencing doubt right now, and that's okay."

"What if I don't . . . ?"—"I accept that I'm experiencing fear right now, and that's okay."

Play with this and see how simple it is to be aware and to accept.

ACTIONS

Pay attention to what you are doing. Are you procrastinating? Are you spending time complaining with your friends? Are you not going to classes? Are you partying a lot? Are you arguing with your roommate? What state of being are your actions reflecting?

Procrastination may reflect fear.

Complaining may reflect limitation.

Not going to classes may also reflect fear.

Partying a lot may reflect denial.

Arguing with your roommate may reflect need.

You probably won't have to dig too deep in order to identify what state of being you are experiencing. And once you've identified it, all you have to do is accept it!

Please keep in mind, *it's all good!* You are free to experience any state of being. When you are aware and accept the state of being you are experiencing, you are consciously creating your reality.

Remember, if state of being is cause, then you only want to accept your state of being, not the circumstances that surround it. The circumstance exists because of the state of being, and trying to accept the circumstance is like trying to change something just by moving it around. Accept your state of being, knowing that you are now expanding acceptance, which will give you thoughts and ideas on how to deal with your circumstances, whatever they happen to be.

WHAT ABOUT REALITY?

One Saturday afternoon my friend's dad, Jim, asked me what I was doing to overcome my anxiety, a topic I'll come back to later. While I was explaining to him how I was using the Law of Attraction, he stopped me and said, "Wait, what about reality, Sebastian?" I responded, "Well, we create our own realities. We get to decide whether or not we want to have a good day or a bad day. We get to decide if we are going to ace the exam, finish the paper on time, and rock the presentation."

Reality is now, not the past or the future. A famous eighteenth-century English poet by the name of William Blake once said, "What is now proved was once only imagined." When the Wright brothers (Wilbur and Orville) told their friends and family they were going to build a piece of machinery to fly in the air, I wonder what their friends and family told them. Wilbur and Orville must have heard things like "Yeah, right," or "That's impossible!" or "You're crazy." In those people's reality, humans flying through the air simply didn't exist as a possibility, but for Wilbur and Orville, it did. They brought their idea to life; they believed in themselves, were willing to consider that they could do it, and they did it. As I tried to explain to my friend's father, we have the ability to change reality in similar ways—we just have to know how to do it.

The next question Jim asked me was "If what you are saying is true, then if I jump off a building and just think positively, are you saying I'll survive?" I told him, "I wouldn't suggest jumping off anything if your current state of being is skepticism that you'll survive." For me, if we are creators, then we create anything. Does that mean I would personally jump off a building? Nope, but I do know people who have walked on 1200-degree coals and not burned their feet. So if we are willing to consciously use the Law of Attraction, we can indeed accomplish feats that right now we consider impossible.

The point I would like to make is this: We can talk about the Law of Attraction until we are blue in the face. The only way you are going to know if it is true for you is by consciously experiencing it. Knowledge is great, but experience is truth. I am not going to tell you that I have all the answers. I am also not going to tell you that what I am inviting you to try will be right for you. What I do know is that my reality changed when I was willing to look beyond it and to consider that I was actually creating it.

Are you willing to look beyond your reality by considering that you have the power to create it? Millions of people are changing their realities by living in the now, using the Law of Attraction, and being positive. I can also tell you that my reality changed one hundred percent when I realized that reality was not something in which I was living, but was, in fact, something I was creating.

Okay, by now you've got the theory down: You are always expanding opportunities to experience more of your current state of being. By being aware of your state of being and accepting whatever it is, you are expanding opportunities to experience more of the states of being that you say you want. Now, it's time to learn how you can use this to deliberately create the college experience you really want!

Chapter 2

DELIBERATELY CREATING WHAT YOU WANT

If one advances confidently in the direction of his dreams, and endeavors to live the life which he has imagined, he will meet with a success unexpected in common hours.

—Henry David Thoreau

What is it you want? When it comes to college, I would imagine that graduating on time, having a great roommate, getting all the classes you want, making your parents proud, having a good time, *and* having a successful academic career would all be at the top of your list. But how do you create all of that while all your focus is on trying to get it all done? Now is a good time to remember the principle behind your ability to create:

You are always creating opportunities to experience more of your current state of being.

To better demonstrate this principle, let's look at an example of a conversation I might have with someone, let's call him Travis, who wants to create a fulfilling, successful academic career.

Me: What do you want to create, Travis?
Travis: I want to create a successful academic career.

Me: Fair enough. What states of being are you going to experience when you have a successful academic career that you're not experiencing today?
Travis: Well, I would probably experience happiness, success, relief, and accomplishment.

Me: Okay. But if creating a successful academic career doesn't bring you the experience of happiness, success, relief, and accomplishment, would you still want a successful academic career?
Travis: I think so, yeah, I mean, I won't be able to get the job I want if I don't do well in college.

Me: What state of being will you experience when you have the job you want?
Travis: Security and wealth, for starters.

Me: So, what you ultimately want is to experience the states of being of happiness, success, relief, accomplishment, security, and wealth.
Travis: I guess so.

Me: So, if a successful academic career doesn't ultimately bring you the experience of happiness, success, relief, accomplishment, or, later—when you get the job you want—security and wealth, would there be any reason to want it?

Travis: I guess not.

Me: Think about it for a second. Where do those states of being exist? In other words, where do you experience them?

Travis: Inside of me.

Me: Exactly. So what you are saying right now is that you *need* a successful academic career in order to experience the states of being of happiness, success, relief, accomplishment, security, and wealth, which actually exist inside of you right now. What is your state of being right now?

Travis: Need.

Me: So what are you creating right now?

Travis: More opportunities to experience need.

Me: Exactly! So the first thing you want to do is accept that you are experiencing need right now, and remind yourself that that's okay. Once you've done that, you'll want to be willing to consider that you *don't need* anything external to you in order to experience the states of being of happiness, success, relief, accomplishment, security, and wealth right this very second. The more you are willing to experience them, the more you are creating opportunities to manifest them in your physical world. If you become willing to experience them now instead of deferring them to an unknown future, then your feelings, thoughts, words, and actions will begin to reflect these states of being. This is how you communicate with your creation partner. Now it just has to bring you all the things *you think* will expand the states of being of happiness, success, relief, accomplishment, and security in your physical world, which would include, in this case, a successful academic career!

Travis: Pretty cool . . .

Me: Now, what do you do when you are not experiencing happiness, success, relief, accomplishment, security, and wealth? You accept whatever state of being you are experiencing.

This is what keeps you open and receptive to the experience of happiness, success, relief, accomplishment, security, and wealth that you've been wanting all this time. What's even cooler is that you don't have to keep your attention on all your wants, just your state of being!

Travis: So all I have to do is know what state of being I'm going to experience when I get the thing I want and be willing to experience it right now and then I will get the thing? It seems so simple!

FOUR STEPS TO DELIBERATELY CREATE WHAT YOU WANT

Let's take all that you've learned so far and break it down into four simple steps, which will become your *creation formula*:

1. Know what you don't want.

2. Know what you ultimately want.

3. Get into the feeling place of your ultimate want.

4. Allow your physical want to come into your experience.

At this point, I invite you to grab a piece of paper and follow along as we take a closer look at each of these steps:

Know What You Don't Want

After everything you've read so far, you may be thinking it doesn't make much sense for you to focus attention on what you don't want. You are absolutely correct. After all, as we've seen, by focusing on what we don't want, we actually create more opportunities to experience that state of want/need/lack. When asked what we want, however, a lot of us respond reflexively with something like "Well, I'll tell you what I don't want . . ." It seems to be in our nature to go straight to the negative.

This is not to say that identifying what we don't want is an exercise in futility, or completely counterproductive to our best interests. The bottom line is that knowing what you *don't* want makes it easy to identify what you *do* want. With that in mind, take a few minutes to identify the things that you don't want. Write them down. Here are a few examples to get you started:

"I don't want to fail."

"I don't want to graduate late."

"I don't want to be stressed out all the time."

"I don't want to my parents to be upset with me."

Write down as many of these as you can come up with (but make sure you are being honest with yourself and staying true to your own personal experience). Once you're ready, move on to step two.

Know What You Ultimately Want

Now that you have a list of your "don't wants," change each one to its inverse, a *"want."* For example:

"I want to pass."

"I want to graduate on time with my friends."

"I want college to be easy."

"I want my parents to be proud of me."

You get the idea. Go ahead and convert your list.

Now it's time to identify what you ultimately want, the state of being you want to experience. What states of being will you experience when you:

Pass with flying colors?

Graduate with all your friends?

Have a fun and easy college experience?

Hear your parents say, "We're so proud of you!"?

Are you going to experience happiness, joy, accomplishment, success, wealth, abundance, security, and confidence? Go ahead and get clear on those states of being.

Get into the Feeling Place of Your Ultimate Want

To get there, you're going to accept that you are experiencing need and be willing to consider that you don't need anything in order to experience the states of being you want right now:

"I accept that I am experiencing need right now, and that's okay. I'm willing to consider that I don't need anything in order to experience [insert state of being you want] right now."

Accepting that you are experiencing need and being willing to consider that you need nothing opens you up to the actual experience of the states of being you identified.

Now you will more easily experience the feelings of happiness, excitement, pride, accomplishment, joy, and so on. Take some time to fully experience these states of being and then, once you have done so, be willing to do the following.

Allow Your Physical Want to Come into Your Experience

This is where the rubber meets the road. It is a good first step to know what we don't want and then to convert that negative into our ultimate, positive want. It is also great to start to experience the feeling state associated with what we want, so that we can begin to generate the energy required to create it.

All of this is good, productive stuff, but we can't stop there. What allows the physical want to actually come into your experience is your willingness to be consciously aware of what you are experiencing *right now and accept whatever it is*. This is how you stay open to your creation partner working with you to bring into your experience all that you want.

So, here you are. You know what you don't want: to fail. You change that into an ultimate want: to pass and to experience the state of being of success. You get into the feeling place by accepting that you are experiencing need and by being willing to consider that you don't need anything in order to experience success right now. If at this stage of the game, like many of us, you start to unconsciously experience your fear of failing again, guess what you are creating? Opportunities to fail!

Think of energy; it is always present. If you spend half an hour, let's say, doing the first three steps, you need to spend the remainder of your waking hours being consciously aware of your state of being, then accept it and gently be willing to consider that you *can* experience the state of being you ultimately want. It may seem daunting to be *consistently* aware of your current state of being and accept it. This is something that takes practice, and even with *lots* of practice your consciousness will still be distracted at times and need to be refocused. The point is simply to realize that the fourth step is where it's at; this is what you need to be mindful of. When you are, you will really experience that right now, at this very moment, you already *have* what it is that you ultimately want.

Let's look at a potential scenario that can arise here. Say you've done your three steps and you then find yourself having the thought, "What if I don't pass?" If you are conscious of it, you will see that this thought is a reflection of the state of being of resistance. Simply accept that you are experiencing resistance right now and assure yourself that that's okay (because it is!). Only then can you be willing to consider what you really want to believe: "I'm willing to consider that I could pass all my finals easily." This leaves you open to attracting what you want and is what allows your creation partner to bring it into your physical experience!

BE WILLING TO CONSIDER

What makes the difference between the two thoughts "I think I can" and "I think I can't"? Your willingness to think them! As I mentioned before, I am not inviting you to fake a state of being that you're not actually experiencing. What do I mean then? Let's say you want to take a specific class to keep your credits on target for graduation. You know this is a popular class and before you even get online to register, you have the thought, "This class will be filled. I'll never get in." If I asked you to change that thought and say, "I know I will get into this class," would you believe yourself? Probably not, but what if I asked you to be willing to consider that it's possible that you could get in? Would you be able to get behind that? This is important because if you say something you don't believe, your state of being is resistance and you end up expanding resistance. If you are willing to consider something, then your state of being is acceptance and you are expanding acceptance and are open to a new possibility. Using our method, then, the thought "I can't" becomes "I'm willing *to consider* that I could." See how simple and easy that is? It's like cracking a window in your mind that allows the state of being of acceptance to expand. It's also the way to eliminate some of the beliefs you've been living with that aren't actually serving you.

Take a second to ask yourself if you really want to believe that there's too much competition, that midterms are a killer, that you won't get the class you want, or that you'll never finish your paper. I'd be willing to bet these are not things you'd choose to believe, but things you reflexively allow yourself to believe just for lack of a better alternative. If you would rather believe something else—the positive inverse of any of these things, for example—all you have to do is simply be willing to *consider* it a possibility. Since you've already accepted the states of being that create those beliefs in the first place—limitation, struggle, and lack—you can now be willing to consider something new. Old, counterproductive ways of thinking give way to new, energizing thoughts. Using this step, watch how the following thoughts get transformed:

"There is too much competition to get into the college I want" becomes *"I'm willing to consider that I could get into the college I want."*

"Midterm exams are a killer" becomes *"I'm willing to consider that I could pass all my exams."*

"That class will fill before I get online to register for it" becomes *"I'm willing to consider that I could get the class I want."*

"I'm never going to finish this term paper" becomes *"I'm willing to consider that I have plenty of time to finish this term paper."*

What state of being is reflected by your new belief? Freedom, possibility, limitlessness, and so on.

One particular semester, I seemed to have a ton of papers due all around the same time, and because of the way my courses worked out, I had to write several of them simultaneously. The thought "What if I don't make the deadlines?" seemed to be playing in my head on repeat. Since I was aware of and was implementing the principles of the Law of Attraction in my life, however, I knew what to do next. First and foremost, I accepted the state of being that was reflected by the thought. I said to myself, "I accept that I am experiencing fear right now, and that's okay."

Once I said this, I started to feel some relief. Then I grabbed a fresh page of loose leaf and wrote down the steps, as well as my own responses to them:

Know what you don't want.

"I don't want to miss the deadline for any of my papers."

Know what you ultimately want.

"I want to hand all of my papers in on time and to do well on each of them. When I do, I will experience relief and accomplishment."

Get into the feeling place of your ultimate want.

I accepted that I was experiencing fear and I was willing to consider that I didn't need anything in order to experience relief and accomplishment right now. Then I had the idea to grab several sheets of paper. On each one I put the title of the paper, the due date, and the final grade. This expanded my experience of relief and accomplishment because I imagined them already done (and done well)!

Allow your physical want to come into your experience.

Then I became willing to consider that I made each deadline with ease and I put my attention on being conscious of what I experienced next. When the thought "What if I don't make the deadlines?" came back, I simply accepted that I was experiencing fear and that that was okay. Then I became willing to consider that I could make all the deadlines with ease. As I did the work necessary, I also noticed that other "synchronicities" started happening, like plans changed that ended up giving me more time, or I would accidentally come across a book that shaved hours off my research time. When these things occurred, I knew my creation partner was leading me in the direction of what I wanted. Those deadlines? They were all met with ease!

IS COLLEGE EVEN RIGHT FOR YOU?

Before we go any further with our discussion of the Law of Attraction and how it might be applied to the college experience, we need to pause and address the fact that some of you reading this book may not even be sure that college is right for you at this time. You may at this very moment be asking yourself, "Is college really the right place for me?" There are a lot of young adults out there struggling with this question, and that's okay! The best thing you can do is get really honest with yourself. You may be tempted to answer the question of whether or not college is right for you based on what is expected of you from your parents, family members, friends, and even society at large. But if you answer yes to the question "Is college right for me?" just because you think it's the supposedly correct answer, you are not being honest with yourself. You are letting others and external realities dictate your internal reality, and that is not conducive to getting what *you* ultimately want.

If you're not crystal clear on the answer to the college question, never fear—acceptance and the four steps of deliberate creation are here! When we don't know the answer to what it is we want, we are simply experiencing confusion. If this is the case with you, start by acknowledging and accepting this feeling state: "I accept that I am experiencing confusion right now, and that's okay."

Now, what don't you want? "I don't want to be confused about whether college is for me."

What do you ultimately want? "I want to know whether college is right for me. I ultimately want to experience clarity."

At this point, get into the feeling place of your ultimate want. Accept that you are experiencing need right now and that that's okay. Then be willing to consider that you don't *need* anything in order to experience clarity right now!

Allow your physical want to come into your experience. Be willing to consider that you already know the answer. What do you think we are creating when we say we don't know something? More not knowing. How about when we are willing to consider that we know something? More knowing! It makes sense, doesn't it? Now when you experience doubt and confusion, you can simply accept and be willing to know again.

Since you are experiencing acceptance, composing a "Pros and *Pros* List" may be an action you want to take to expand clarity. Instead of weighing the pros and cons of each result, you can simply focus on the pros of each and choose the option that is most appealing to you. After all, knowing what you now know about the Laws of Attraction, how positive could a "Pros and *Cons* List" ever be?

Let's take a scenario in which you're deciding whether to attend college. Below I've compiled a list of pros about going to college versus a list of pros about not going. (Keep in mind that this can also be applied to the question of whether to remain in college, if this is something you are struggling with.)

Here are some pros about sticking with college:

You will meet new people.

You will party and have a good time.

You will feel independent.

You will take classes you are interested in.

You will expand your knowledge.

You will likely find some direction toward a career path.

Here are a few pros about not going to college:

You will get to start working full-time (and having an income) sooner.

You will have some time to think about what you really want to study, should you later decide to attend.

You will save a lot on college tuition and books.

If you want to start your own business, you can focus your energy entirely on that.

These are just a few examples; obviously, every person's situation is going to be a little different, and every person's reasons for attending or not attending college are different. After looking at your "Pros and Pros List," you should have a better idea of the path that seems more appealing to you. If you have been rigorously honest in creating your lists and if you can be aware of what resonates with you, the next most important thing is just to stay true to yourself. That said, if you've decided that not going to college is the more fitting path for you and find this scary or overwhelming, allow yourself to experience those things fully. Remember, you may think you are letting people down, but believe it or not, you cause a lot more damage to yourself and others if you aren't true to what you really want. In the end, being true to what you want is more important than doing what family or society expects of us, and definitely more important than going along with what's popular. It is so very important to listen to ourselves, be rigorously honest in our decisions, and always go with our hearts.

If you find that you are in the position of thinking college may not be right for you, sit down with your parents and talk about your options. Go over some scenarios that might fit better with what you want. Try not to think about what others will think of you. Do what is right for *you* and what will make you happy. If you find that you're experiencing pressure, accept it and be honest about it! Ask for more time. Remember, it really doesn't matter what you *decide* as much as it matters what you will *create*.

If, on the other hand, you decide that college *is* for you, then it's time to take all of what you learned so far and apply it to creating the college experience you really want—emotionally, academically, physically, and socially. But first, a lesson on creating more time.

Chapter 3

TIME CAN BE ON YOUR SIDE

*If time flies when
you're having fun,
it hits the afterburners
when you don't think
you're having enough.*

—Jef Mallett

Why do we go to college? Of course we go to learn, but let's be honest here: we go to get a degree that will set us up for a job in a profession that will eventually provide for a lifestyle we have envisioned for ourselves (or, at the very least, pay the bills). To graduate, we need to pass our classes, and to pass our classes, we need to take exams, write papers, create and deliver presentations, and actually show up at our classes, as scheduled.

This all sounds perfectly reasonable until the first day of class when the professor tells you that you have a fifteen-page paper due at the end of each month for the whole semester, while another says your final grade will be based on a single exam that covers all of the course work for the semester, and yet another one says that 50 percent of your grade will be based on an hour-long presentation in front of the entire class. And that's just three out of the five classes you've registered for this semester. If there is one thing you are quickly going to feel you don't have enough of, it's *time*.

Let's consider some common axioms about time:

"There are only twenty-four hours in a day."

"Time is running out."

"There is never enough time."

"You have to manage your time."

"Time is short."

"Time is money."

"Time is not your friend."

With these beliefs, it's no wonder so many of us say things like:

"I do not have any time to do that."

"Where did my day go? It went so fast."

"I wish I had time to do that."

"I am too busy to help."

"I can't. I don't have the time."

"I never have enough time."

With these beliefs and the workload you've just been handed, is it any wonder you are experiencing "not enough" of the one thing you need the most—time?

CREATING TIME

Managing your time is helpful if you are going to get this all done on time to the standards your professors require. At the end of this chapter, I will share some positive actions for managing your time, which will help you be more efficient. Keep this in mind, though: managing your time is great, but it can't give you the experience that you could actually have more than enough time to get everything done. Why? Because when you say you don't have enough time, you are actually expanding opportunities to experience *lack,* no matter how efficient you get at managing your time.

This gets back to an idea we've touched on that is fundamental to the Law of Attraction: when you say you don't have enough of anything—money, love, happiness, time, and so on—you are experiencing a state of being of lack. If you are experiencing lack, particularly with time, then it will not be possible for you to experience an abundance of it because you are actually expanding opportunities to experience greater *lack* of it. If you want to experience an abundance of time, you will need to accept that you are experiencing the state of being of lack. Only then can you be willing to consider a new possibility. Acceptance is the key.

Try telling yourself: "I accept that I am experiencing lack right now, and that's okay."

Now deliberately create what you want:

Know what you don't want.
" I don't want to run out of time."

Know what you ultimately want.
" I want to have plenty of time to get everything done and have fun with my friends. When I do I will experience relief, happiness, and freedom."

Get into the feeling place of your ultimate want.
Be willing to consider that you don't need anything in order to experience relief, happiness, and freedom right now. Identify how you will feel when you have all the time in the world, when all this work is easily completed and you are hanging out with your friends.

Allow your physical want to come into your experience.
When you experience lack, accept it, and be willing to know that you can have plenty of time to get everything done. You might say: "I am willing to consider that I have more than enough time right now."

Let's take a second to see if this resonates.

Say to yourself, "I don't have enough time."

Now say, "I am willing to consider that I have more than enough time."

Which statement *feels* better? Which one do you really want to believe? Do you really want to believe you don't have enough time or would you rather believe that you have more than enough? Remember, when you say that you don't have enough time, you are expanding opportunities to experience "not enough time." When you are willing to consider that you have more then enough time, you are opening yourself up to a new possibility and are therefore creating in the direction of "having more than enough time."

The other day I was out doing errands when I realized I had lost track of time. I was ten minutes from a scheduled meeting and had only five minutes to get there. My first thought was "I'm never going to make it." But I remembered the steps and accepted that I was experiencing lack and that that was okay. I then became willing to consider that I had more than enough time to get home. I got in the car and started out.

As I was driving, I realized I wasn't rushing. I actually found myself taking my time, which makes sense, if you think about it, because a person who has more than enough time doesn't have to rush. When I got behind a slow-moving car, I simply accepted what I was experiencing—frustration—and was again willing to consider that I had more than enough time. I also noticed that I wasn't looking at the clock—why would I do that if time is on my side? Before long, I drove into my driveway, parked my car, and looked at the time. Only six minutes had passed! What normally took ten minutes only took me six minutes. Do I think I created four minutes? You bet I do. And you can, too!

Remember, your energy or state of being is constantly creating. When you are willing to consider that you have more than enough time, you are creating opportunities to experience an abundance of time. If you are experiencing not enough, you are really just creating opportunities to experience a lack of time; your creation partner can and does respond to your state of being. In the end, for all of us, it comes down to a matter of choice: Do I want to experience lack or abundance? It's your choice, but no matter which one you go with, your reality will start reflecting the one you are expanding, *always*!

WHERE ARE YOU LIVING?

Have you ever spent time with an infant? Infants live in one place and one place only: *the now*. They do not know anything about the past or the future. They live fully and completely each second of their life because that is simply all they know. Ignorance is bliss, right? Well, the truth is that you could experience the same bliss if you became willing to live in the only time that ever really exists—the present. Imagine not regretting the past or fretting about the future, but just enjoying the moment.

Since grammar school, we've been taught that time is linear, and most of our academic attention is focused on the past. In history class, we're taught the concept of time by using timelines to map human progress—the medieval age preceded the Renaissance, which was followed by the Reformation, which preceded the Age of Enlightenment, and so on. And while our minds are wrapping themselves around the past—from historical timelines to literary movements to scientific discoveries—we are constantly being shaped and readied for an unknown future (elementary school leads to middle school, which is followed by high school, then college, and so on). It's no wonder that so many of us struggle to stay attuned to the present, when most of our lives have been spent training our minds to chart out the past and anticipate the future.

As we get into the groove of college, we can find ourselves bombarded with negative, draining thoughts about our personal past—nostalgia, longing for an identity we had in high school that suddenly seems uncertain, academic and social regrets. We can also feel weighed down by anxieties concerning the future: What do I want to major in? What do I want to do with my degree? Will I meet my future husband/wife in school? What happens if I don't?

With all of this going on in our heads, it's no wonder we don't feel we're in control.

Think about it for a second: How much of your day do you spend focused solely on the moment? If you're like most people, probably very little. We all seem compelled to ruminate over the past or anticipate the future at the expense of our engagement with the now. We try to control something that already happened, or something that we think will happen, rarely, if ever, reminding ourselves that we can't do either. If this moment is the only thing that really exists, then it is the only point of time over which we have any control. So, if you want to be in control, be willing to be in the moment.

That said, a lot of us are "trying" to be in the moment by concentrating on the physical reality that surrounds us. That's fine, but remember what is actually being created: your state of being, which exists not outside of you, but inside of you. So, being in the moment is not about noticing your environment; it's about being aware of the state of being you are experiencing and accepting whatever it is.

I know this can all be difficult to absorb because it is so different from what you've been conditioned to believe, but let's just see if it resonates with you. Ask yourself:

"Is it easier to pay attention to everything in front of me, or would it be easier to only have to pay attention to what is inside of me, my state of being?"

For me, it was easier to keep my attention on one thing as opposed to many things. Since that was the case, I was willing to consider that my time was better spent on being aware of my state of being and accepting whatever it was. I also realized that the only thing that actually exists right now is our current experience. As soon as we think, say, do, or even observe something, it is in the past. The only thing that remains constant is our experience in this moment, our state of being.

When your attention is on your state of being, then you are automatically in the moment because you are dealing with the only thing that exists right now: your current experience. So what happens when you drift into the past or barrel toward the future? You get caught in patterns of thought that keep you from being in the moment. When that happens, you're likely to feel frustrated, anxious, and defeated. The next time you catch yourself thinking about the past or future, be willing to pay attention to your thoughts and ask yourself what state of being they are reflecting, and then truly accept that state of being for what it is. For example:

For thoughts regarding the past:

"I really miss my high school" becomes *"I accept that I'm experiencing sadness right now, and that's okay."*

"If only I hadn't failed that test" becomes *"I accept that I'm experiencing regret right now, and that's okay."*

"I wish I had done better on the assignment" becomes *"I accept that I'm experiencing judgment right now, and that's okay."*

For thoughts regarding the future:

"What if I don't pass the exam on Friday?" becomes *"I accept that I'm experiencing fear right now, and that's okay."*

"What if I don't get the class I want?" becomes *"I accept that I'm experiencing limitation right now, and that's okay."*

"I'm never going to get this paper done on time" becomes *"I accept that I'm experiencing worry right now, and that's okay."*

Welcome to the moment! If you are aware of your state of being, you are automatically in the moment (the present). If you accept your current state of being rather than resist it, you are then creating a new moment that is in alignment with what you say you want.

WHAT IS ACTUALLY HAPPENING HERE?

When we say we don't have enough time, what do we typically do? We make choices that support the fact that we don't have enough time. The thoughts in our head go something like this: "Since I don't have enough time to get the paper done anyway, I'll just watch one more TV show. I'll just get done what I can get done and that will have to be enough." Notice how the thoughts and actions are expanding "not enough" and are in alignment with not getting the paper done?

Now if we are willing to consider that we have more than enough time, the thoughts in our head will probably go something like this: "Since I have more than enough time to get this paper done, I'll finish it up and record the TV show I wanted to watch. I'll have plenty of time to watch it after the paper is done, maybe even later tonight." Now the thoughts and actions are expanding "more than enough" and are in alignment with getting the paper done.

Remember, you are always creating opportunities to experience more of your current state of being. This state of being becomes a physical reality through your feelings, thoughts, words, and actions. Simply put, your state of being of "more than enough" expands into feelings of abundance and abundant thoughts, words, actions, and physical reality. You start to notice how the physical world actually supports your state of being. Let me give you an example of what happened when I became aware of my state of being, accepted it, and was willing to consider that I could have more than enough time.

My junior year of college I took a sociology class. I was excited about the class until I got the reading assignment—one book a week! I immediately started to experience stress and was instantly over-whelmed. How was I going to have enough time to read a book a week in addition to all my other assignments? I knew I was experiencing lack and stress and was therefore creating opportunities to experience more of the same. It was time to use the four steps to start creating in the direction I really wanted. I took out a piece of loose leaf and started deliberately creating. First, as always, I accepted what I was experiencing and then I applied the steps to my experience.

"I accept that I'm experiencing lack and overwhelm right now, and that's okay."

Know what you don't want.
"I don't want to fall behind in my assigned reading."

Know what you ultimately want.
"I want to have more than enough time to read all my assignments. When I do, I will experience accomplishment and relief."

Get into the feeling place of your ultimate want.
I was willing to consider that I didn't need anything in order to experience accomplishment and relief right now. Then I pictured myself hanging out on the quad, reading and relaxing.

Allow your physical want to come into your experience.
When the state of being of lack or stress came up, I accepted it and was willing to consider that I could have more than enough time to complete my reading assignments.

Some interesting things started to happen that had to be the work of my creation partner. My sociology professor did not get to all of the books he planned that semester. My reading assignments for his class were significantly reduced. Another professor did not hold class for six sessions and so the reading got bumped to a report. I ended up dropping one course and picked up a course that, unbeknownst to me, had no reading assignments. Turns out these changes created more than enough time for me to complete my reading assignments with ease. My willingness to experience accomplishment and relief created a physical reality where I could actually sit in the quad, relax, and enjoy my reading assignments!

So, remember to do your part, accept what you are experiencing, and be willing to consider that you have more than enough time. Then watch how not only your feelings, thoughts, words, and actions start to align with what you want, but how physical reality does as well!

POSITIVE ACTIONS

Now that you are aware and consciously creating time, here are some positive actions you can take that are in alignment with you continuing to create more time and getting done what you want to get done. Remember, these are suggestions, so read them and see which ones resonate with you. Then give them a try.

Designate Your Time

Academic Time—Take time each day (that includes weekends) to devote to your academics. During this time, just be sure that you are doing something that will help move you closer to completing your assignments, even if it means just a little bit of reading/writing/researching at a time. Everybody studies effectively at different times, so work this time in when it feels right for you, not just when you think you should be doing it.

"Me Time"—This is specific time that is devoted to whatever it is you want to do. If you want to watch a movie, go to the beach, read a book, wash your car, or play a sport, then do it. Some of us tend to feel guilty taking time for ourselves. It would be an awful waste if you spent your "Me Time" worrying about all the other things you think you should be doing. When we don't do what we want and only focus on what we "should" be doing, we start to experience resentment. When we experience resentment, then we are expanding opportunities to experience resentment and, along with that, more "shoulds." When we do things we enjoy, we experience happiness, so we are expanding opportunities to experience more happiness! If, while taking this time for yourself, you do experience guilt or worry, accept that you are experiencing them and that it is okay. Then be willing to consider that it is actually important for you to take time for yourself.

Family and Friends Time—This is time when you just hang out with your family or your friends and do nothing else. Spending time with people you love expands your experience of happiness, so turn off your cell phones, get off your computers, put away your schoolwork, and talk with those who mean the most to you. Share stories, play games, go out on the town, or work on a creative project together.

Silent Time—With all the noise we encounter in our daily lives, silence is of the utmost importance. Noise expands opportunities to experience chaos. Silence expands opportunities to experience peace. Take some time to relax your mind and simply sit in silence. Find a spot that will be completely quiet. A room, your car, outside at a park will work—any place that is sure to be very quiet. When you turn down the noise, you'll notice that your mind gets louder. Listen to your thoughts and just accept the state of being they are reflecting. If you keep accepting, you will notice that your thoughts slow down and then they aren't even there anymore. Now you can really enjoy the silence.

TV Time—Ever pay attention to how you feel after you watch something on TV? Now that you are starting to become aware of your state of being, you will probably notice that certain programs leave you feeling great while others leave you feeling blah. I started to notice several things about my own TV viewing:

Watching sports—felt great

Watching the news—not so great

Funny and inspiring movies—felt great

Reality TV—not so great

What do you watch on TV? How do you feel after watching it? There was a time when I was watching *The Jerry Springer Show* on a fairly regular basis; I got hooked on the excitement, the drama, and the inevitable brawls that would break out onstage. As I was practicing the steps, however, I started to notice that when the show was over, I felt pretty awful. Something in my body just did not feel right. On the other hand, when I watched a series called *Planet Earth* on the Discovery channel, documenting the wonder of Earth and all the amazing things that live on it, I felt great! I would just sit on my couch in amazement and appreciation for the complex, natural world in which we live. I could feel myself swelling with more knowledge, not depleting with all the backstabbing, drama, cheap shots, and other stuff always showcased on Jerry Springer.

As you start expanding your experience of abundance, happiness, and fun, you will start to notice that you will also choose not to watch the old "negative" programs you may have enjoyed in the past.

Here's a way you can be sure if a program is in alignment with what you want. Simply ask yourself, "How do I think I will feel after watching this?" Answer honestly and make your choice. You may know that something will not feel good but you'll decide to watch it anyway. That's perfectly fine; just accept your state of being while you are watching the program. Be sure that you don't waste time beating yourself up afterward for watching something that you may now consider to have been a waste of time. Once you've established a habit of practicing the four steps, you'll find that you naturally gravitate toward things that engage your positivity. Soon you might just turn the channel rather than sit through something that isn't in alignment with what you really want—to feel good!

News: I have an acronym for the news—"Negative Energy with Stories." Watching the news is pretty depressing. Anything scandalous or overtly negative happening in your city, town, country, and world is sure to make its way to the six o'clock news if it's spectacular enough to make for "good" TV. Every day the news broadcasters seem to top their performances of the day before by reporting all the murders, cop shootings, storm disasters, political feuds, and economic losses they could scrounge up. In short, the news is a surefire way to expand your state of being of fear!

Since the news doesn't expand the states of being I choose, I have stopped watching it. Now some of you might say, "But it's important to know what is going on in the world." What's important is for you to be aware of your state of being so you know what you are creating in your world. I'm not suggesting that you stick your head in the sand when it comes to world events, but it is important to recognize that much of the news you watch is sensationalized and designed to expand fear. If you choose to watch it, the opportunity is to be sure that you accept your state of being so that you continue to create in the direction you want.

Commercials: If you want to expand need and fear, continue watching commercials. The messages they feed us are anything but positive. Many have us dying from some dreadful disease and in need of care or legal representation, depressed and in need of medication, in a car accident and in need of auto insurance. Others convince us that we will never be pretty enough, skinny enough, smart enough—until we buy their product, that is.

Ways to bypass these negative, spirit-draining messages are to mute them or to record your favorite shows and fast-forward through the commercials. You'll save about ten minutes for every half-hour show you watch and you won't get caught up in the cycles of negativity and self-loathing that companies spend big bucks to create.

Once you start being aware and accepting of the moment you are in, you will find that the time you used to spend in front of the TV, which used to unconsciously expand fear and lack in you, can now be used to create more life-affirming experiences.

Internet Time—We are bombarded with technology everywhere. At work, at school, at home . . . even at the dentist's office! We certainly benefit from the conveniences it offers, but it also makes us so much more accessible, in a depleting way. The time we had between calls has now been filled with responding to text messages. Technology's promise to give us more time has not come through but resulted in us actually having less. Here are some ways to get that time back:

Make an agreement with yourself on how often you want to spend time checking and responding to e-mail. Maybe three times a day, maybe five? See what works for you and then be willing to give it a try. When you check your e-mail, be sure you have enough time to respond. That way you won't have unanswered messages hanging over your head.

Social networking—Use the "Me Time" mentioned previously for social networking. Try to be sure that you are spending just the right amount of time for you. Pay attention to what you are experiencing so that you know when and how much is enough. Be aware of your state of being. Are you experiencing jealousy and therefore checking up on an ex of yours? Accept that you are experiencing jealousy right now and remind yourself that that's okay. When you do, you won't feel compelled to spend your time checking up on anybody. Are you experiencing need? Do you need friends and therefore spending a lot of time "enhancing" your profile? Accept that you're experiencing need right now; it's okay! Now, operating from a place of acceptance, you'll find you won't need to spend as much time on your profile. It's just a matter of being aware and accepting your state of being. Do these things and you'll end up spending the perfect amount of time social networking.

Browsing—*Be sure you have a reason to go online and then be willing to stick with that reason. It is so easy to get off track but just as easy to get back on by checking in with yourself. Every once in a while, just ask yourself if you are still on task. If not, bookmark what you are looking at and get back on task.*

Cell phones—*Turn them off during your designated times. Interruptions can turn into a huge waste of time if we are not aware. Be sure when you turn it back on that you have the time to return your calls and texts.*

Gamers—*Take breaks, go for walks, and get away from the game for a while. You will find that ten- to twenty-minute breaks between games will not only make you physically feel better, but it will also make you play better!*

More important than all these practical suggestions is your willingness to be aware and accept your current state of being so that you are always creating in the direction of what you ultimately want. Without awareness and acceptance, implementing any of the suggestions will help you manage your time, but alone they will never create the experience of having more than enough time.

Chapter 4

THE EMOTIONAL RESULTS YOU WANT

Feelings are like toes!
They have to breathe free or
they'll stink to high heaven!

—Takayuki Ikkaku,
Arisa Hosaka,
and Toshihiro Kawabata
(*Animal Crossing: Wild World*, 2005)

What is the one thing that cuts across all areas of your life—your academic, financial, social, and physical worlds? YOU! You don't wake up every morning and quarter yourself and go live your day in different parts, with different selves. You, and you alone, experience every part of your life. As I hope you are starting to see, you are not passively experiencing these parts of your life; you are actively creating every one of those areas, whether you like it or not.

You are always creating opportunities to experience more of your current state of being. This state of being is becoming a physical experience through feelings, thoughts, words, actions, and your perception of your physical reality. So your state of being is causing your feelings, thoughts, words, actions, and perception of physical reality. Therefore feelings, thoughts, words, actions, and your perception of reality are all effects of your current state of being.

It will be hard for you to manage your academic demands if you aren't able to manage the emotional and physical demands (of which there are many!) of being in college. For starters, there's the homesickness, with which many of you may be struggling. It's natural to miss your home, to miss all that has been done for you in the past, your friends (some of whom you've probably known your whole life), your social status in high school class, and, basically, your old life! Who wouldn't feel some sense of loss, some longing for the familiar in the face of so much change—your new home (which probably amounts to nothing more than a twelve-by-fifteen-foot dorm room), new roommate, new schedule, new expectations, and all the many new faces and dynamics you're taking in every day? Is it any big surprise that once you've attended even your first five classes, you experience pressure, stress, anxiety, worry, fear, panic, and even doubt that you will survive your new life? Absolutely not!

Remember you are the experiencer, not the experience. This is very important to remember as you either start or continue your college experience. Why? Because you will be tempted to look out at your reality and judge yourself according to what you see, and when you do, according to the principles of the Law of Attraction, you will just be creating opportunities to experience more of the same!

I am here to tell you that you are *not* a loser because you failed an exam, dropped a course, missed a class, got a D on your paper, got drunk and made a fool of yourself, or bounced a check because of the zero funds in your bank account. Those are all just physical experiences that you, as the experiencer, experienced. Of course, some of you may never fail an exam, drop a course, get a D, get drunk, or bounce a check, but even for those of you who are seemingly on top of things, college may be a struggle. You might consider yourself weak, for example, because you miss your home, parents, friends, high school, and previous life. Remember, you are not weak; you are just the experiencer, experiencing the states of being of weakness, sadness, and loss.

As the experiencer, you are free to experience any state of being, including weakness, failure, embarrassment, sadness, and loss. This might seem to contradict what you've learned about dealing with your emotions in the past. You've probably been encouraged to ignore, shut out, push down, or even deny what you are feeling, especially if it's unpleasant. It has also probably been suggested by family, friends, and society at large that you not talk about any of these negative emotions or, heaven forbid, outwardly display them. Take a close look at the implications of this unspoken expectation. Do you think it encourages you to experience the state of being of *acceptance* or of *resistance*? You got it—resistance. What happens, in your experience, when you try to ignore or resist what you are feeling? I would bet that, like me, you start to experience more of it. The more you resist what you are experiencing, the bigger it gets. Remember, "What you resist persists." Man, is that the truth. And that's the Law of Attraction at work. It's just manifesting the results you don't want!

USING YOUR EMOTIONS AS YOUR CREATION TOOL

When we suppress our feelings/emotions, we miss an important opportunity to be aware and accept our current state of being.

Having the perception that our feelings are actually a tool meant to point us back to our current state of being so we can accept it keeps us creating in the direction we really want. How can you use your emotions as a tool instead of letting them dictate your experience? First, remember that feelings/emotions are the physical reflections of a state of being. A happy feeling is a reflection of a state of being of happiness. An angry feeling is a reflection of a state of being of anger. Since state of being is cause, we want to remember that the feeling is the effect, then we can use the feeling/emotion to point us back to the state of being—cause—so we can accept it. Before we can experience success, we have to be aware that we are experiencing a feeling of failure first. Only when we accept that as our experience can we then become open to experiencing success.

Say you don't do as well on your midterm as you had wanted. A feeling of failure comes over you. Look at that feeling and ask yourself, "What state of being am I experiencing right now?" Identify the feeling—failure. Now it's time to move into acceptance: "I accept that I'm experiencing failure right now, and that's okay." This is not about accepting that you didn't do well on your midterm, this is about accepting *the state of being of failure* so that you can start to expand opportunities to *experience acceptance*, which would include thoughts about what could be possible for you, like experiencing success so that next time you ace your exam.

When you think about home and you feel homesick, you might ask yourself, "What state of being am I experiencing right now?" If "sadness" is your answer, say this to yourself (and mean it!): "I accept that I'm experiencing sadness right now, and that's okay."

Let's say you had a few too many beers last night and you embarrassed yourself, or let's say you had intended to study for a big test coming up, but got sucked into TV instead. When you think about what you did and you feel regret, go through this inner dialogue with yourself: "What state of being am I experiencing right now? Regret. I accept that I am experiencing regret right now, and that's okay."

What is happening here? When you take your attention off the circumstance (the effect) and put it on the state of being (the cause), you are consciously creating a new moment with new circumstances. You are now able to deal with the circumstance you are in from a state of being of *acceptance,* which is in alignment with what you ultimately want: to experience success, happiness, and forgiveness. Now your feelings, thoughts, words, and actions will start to expand opportunities to experience more of these states of being.

The proof is in your experience, so give this a try right now. What are you experiencing right now? Maybe some newfound clarity, maybe confusion, maybe even some skepticism that this stuff really works. Whatever it is that you are feeling right now, accept it all and be willing to see what happens next.

Remember that you are the experiencer *having* an experience; you are not the *experience!* As the experiencer, you are not:

Angry

Frustrated

A failure

An embarrassment

You *are* the experiencer experiencing a state of being of:

Anger

Frustration

Failure

Embarrassment

Declare each of these phrases out loud and pay close attention to what physically happens after you say each one:

"I am a failure."

"I am experiencing a state of being of failure."

What did you feel in your body? Which one made you feel resistance? Which one made you feel acceptance?

Personally, I experience acceptance when I say, "I am experiencing a state of being of [insert whatever that feeling is]." As the experiencer, I feel as though I have a choice over what happens next. When I say, "I am a failure," in that moment I have no choice; I *am* a failure. Wouldn't you always rather have a choice and thus feel in control?

WHAT DO YOU DO WHEN YOU FEEL *REALLY* BAD?

Ever have those times when your mind is racing, you feel anxious, and it seems like the more you try to control this experience, the more you seem to spiral further into it? I know sometimes I feel like the only way to stop the spiral is to put my head through a wall. Of course, I don't actually do this, but sometimes it feels like that would be the only relief.

As you play with the acceptance of your state of being, sometimes you will immediately start to experience states of relief, peace, and happiness. Sometimes you won't even remember what you were upset about even a minute later. Sometimes you will have an insight, and a whole new perspective about your circumstance will come rushing into your consciousness. Other times your experience won't be quite so immediate, but that's completely okay.

When you are experiencing what you might consider extreme fear, frustration, or anger, stay present with your experience and allow yourself to accept and listen, accept and listen, accept and listen.

Here's an example.

You have the thought: "I miss my old life."

ACCEPT: "I accept that I'm experiencing loss right now, and that's okay."
LISTEN: Pay attention to what is going on inside of you, listen to your feelings and thoughts.

Another thought comes in: "How am I ever going to manage college on my own?"

ACCEPT: "I accept that I'm experiencing limitation right now, and that's okay."
LISTEN

The next thought comes in: "I'm so tired of feeling alone."

ACCEPT: "I accept that I'm experiencing loneliness right now, and that's okay."
LISTEN

Next thought: "I'm sooooo tired of accepting."

ACCEPT: "I accept that I'm experiencing frustration right now, and that's okay."
LISTEN

ACCEPT

LISTEN

ACCEPT

At some point, you'll notice that your thoughts will begin to change automatically and will start reflecting acceptance. Now you are open to the willingness to consider something new (which is a crucial part of the process). Before you know it, your thoughts will become something like: "I'm willing to consider that I could experience happiness right now." Not only will you think this, you will actually *feel* happy!

Doreen, the coauthor of this book, shared the following example of what happened when she was spiraling and willing to stick with acceptance:

> Someone who had hurt me deeply in the past said something to me that brought all the old thoughts and feelings rushing back. My mind was racing with thoughts like "How could she have done that to me? Why did she do that to me? I can't believe she did that to me." All that I had learned about state of being and acceptance went flying out the window and I just spiraled. I was experiencing anxiousness, panic, abandonment, anger, jealousy, rage, and hatred. Physically, my stomach ached, my blood was rushing, and I started to get a headache (which I never get). I was going down fast!

> At some point, I did come to my senses and I started accepting and accepting and accepting and accepting. I was still experiencing the states of being and it seemed as though my thoughts and headache were expanding, but I just kept on accepting, and then accepting some more. All of a sudden the thought came in, "I know that acceptance will get me where I want to go, but why do I have to suffer so much?" Then, like a ton of bricks it hit me, "You are not suffering, you are experiencing a state of being of suffering!"

Immediately upon having this thought, I experienced peace. My thoughts cleared, my stomach was calm, my blood stopped rushing, and my headache disappeared! I stuck with acceptance and it expanded into an insight that changed my whole perspective and left me in a state of being of peace.

Think of your occasional emotional/mental spirals as a rope with knots in it. Each knot represents a state of being that you simply want to accept. At some point you come to the end of the rope, which means there are no more knots and you realize that everything really is okay. At this point, you will begin to feel that you can handle this college experience just fine. You'll even start to have ideas on how you can do just that.

Remember, the state of being of acceptance opens you up to the world where all the powerful positive states of being that you ultimately want to experience are actually waiting to be experienced by you. So it stands to reason that the more you accept, the more you expand all that you want to experience. So, *again,* acceptance is the key!

Depression/Anxiety

According to HealthyMinds.org, "One out of four young adults will experience a depressive episode by age twenty-four." It also reports, "Nearly half of all college students report feeling so depressed at some point in time that they have trouble functioning." This should come as no surprise. Who wouldn't experience depression in the face of all the many changes college brings, coupled with the huge amount of responsibility it demands?

Resistance to depression will only expand opportunities to experience depression. If you are experiencing depression, you may not want to admit that you are, which is, as you know, resistance. Try to remember that you are not weak because you are experiencing depression; you are just *experiencing* a state of being of depression. And, as we've been practicing, as the experiencer, you can treat depression just like any other state of being. Accept it: "I accept that I am experiencing depression right now, and that's okay."

When you allow yourself to accept depression and continue to accept it, then you'll know what you want to do about it. Maybe you'll want to talk with someone about it. If that is the case, there are a multitude of opportunities right on your college campus for you to receive help. Of course, you can also turn to your family. When you are in a state of being of acceptance, you will be willing to seek out help and be better able to choose the best plan for you.

Whether you are experiencing depression, anxiety, panic, fatigue, or fear, your first opportunity is to accept that you are the experiencer experiencing a state of being and remind yourself that it's okay. Only then can you begin to get an idea of what you want to deliberately create next.

I began experiencing severe anxiety attacks a few months before my high school graduation. I guess it stemmed from being nervous about going to college, leaving home, and starting a new phase in my life. It was all just so overwhelming. I had never had an anxiety attack before, and as I approached graduation the attacks seemed to grow increasingly worse.

When I got to college, I started to experience all that I had feared, so the attacks got even worse. I remember sitting in bed one night, experiencing such severe panic that I felt like my entire body was being held down against my will, and I didn't have the energy to overcome it. Tears were running down my face as I asked myself, "Why is my life being controlled by anxiety? Why now, in college, which everyone had always told me would be the best experience of my life?" As the attacks continued, they caused damage to my friendships, to my relationship with my girlfriend, and even to my health. I reached a point where I had experienced enough. They say when your back is pushed against the wall, you either "go insane" or "become a mystic." Frankly, I wasn't ready to go insane, and I certainly wasn't convinced that I wanted to be a mystic either. I just wanted to feel *free*.

More to the point, I also knew that I didn't want to have to leave college (which was becoming a possibility). Having had some exposure to the principles of the Law of Attraction, I knew that I had to put acceptance and those four steps of deliberate creation into action, and I needed to do it immediately or I was going to ruin any chance of being a college graduate. I grabbed a pen and piece of paper, sat down on my dorm bed, and put the four steps into action. Here is what I wrote:

"I accept that I am experiencing anxiety right now, and that's okay." As soon as I established this acceptance, even on paper, suddenly all the "whys" I had been asking didn't seem to matter as much. All that mattered was that I recognized what I was experiencing and could start to get into a place of acceptance.

Know what you don't want.

"I don't want to have to leave college because of these anxiety attacks."

Know what you ultimately want.

"I want to be anxiety-free and graduate college with my girlfriend. When I do, I will experience freedom and accomplishment."

Get into the feeling place of your ultimate want.

I was willing to consider that I didn't need anything in order to experience freedom and accomplishment right now. When I did, I started to feel better and was even able to picture my girlfriend and me taking photos after graduation. I saw both our families surrounding and hugging us and offering their congratulations. I even pictured the black robe I'd be wearing and how silky it felt. I felt the diploma being handed to me and the tickle of the tassel on my face as I moved it to the other side of my cap. Picturing these details gave me entry into the feeling of the moment of that day. The images were so real to me that I got goose bumps.

Allow your physical want to come into your experience.

I continued to accept when I experienced anxiety and was willing to consider that I could graduate anxiety-free. I was willing to allow my creation partner to show me the way, and it did!

Things started to happen after I did this exercise. I noticed that I was able to more comfortably hang out with and get to know my new roommate, Paul. I began to get comfortable with finding my way around the campus; it was starting to feel more like home to me, and not just some alien place I had been plopped into. I started to meet new friends in my classes. I got more and more comfortable with my schoolwork and was even getting some good grades back.

One night on the way back from the library, I suddenly realized something: I hadn't had an anxiety attack in over a month! My thoughts about leaving college and worrying about grades, leaving home, and meeting new people had all disappeared. All the fear and negativity seemed to have vanished. What I was willing to consider was coming true—my college life was indeed turning out pretty great. Leaving home did not seem that bad, after all. I felt strong knowing that I had acceptance and the four steps of deliberate creation to guide me through the other challenges that were bound to come up in my college experience (and even beyond graduation). I had the formula I needed to finally live the life I had always wanted for myself. All I had to do was be sure to continue to consciously apply the steps along the way.

A lot of us are dealing with some pretty intense emotions. The good news is that we are armed with a guiding, empowering principle—we are creators and, as creators, we can't be hindered by anything, including our emotions. If we are willing to accept what we are experiencing, we won't get stuck in these emotions; we will move through them and start to experience states of being we really want to experience. So my invitation to you is to be willing to consider that no matter how anxious, depressed, sad, fearful, or overwhelmed you are right now, you always have within you the power to create something new. Moreover, you now have the formula to effectively use that power!

Chapter 5

THE ACADEMIC RESULTS YOU WANT

Education's purpose is to replace an empty mind with an open one.

—Malcolm Forbes,
Forbes magazine

By this point, you've learned what creates your experience: the state of being you are experiencing in any given moment. You now know that resisting a state of being actually expands it, whereas accepting it leaves you open to experiencing the opposite of whatever state of being you are resisting. You know that your feelings, thoughts, words, and actions are reflections of your current state of being and can be used as tools to make you more aware of your state of being so that you can work on accepting. You know that only when you get into a place of acceptance can you deliberately create what you want. You also know that you can utilize the four steps of deliberate creation to accomplish what you want, while staying emotionally balanced. Armed with this new knowledge, you can now create the college experience you want and deserve!

If you are open to it and willing to practice the principles we've discussed, the Law of Attraction will provide you with a solid foundation for creating your academic world. That's what we are going to focus on in this chapter. I hope that by the end of it, when you think about your academic responsibilities, you will be excited by the prospect of creating, instead of dreading, your final GPA.

GRADES

Our primary objective in college is to graduate with a degree. That's why we go. It seems like a given, but it's easy to lose sight of our mission (one that will have implications for the rest of our adult lives) in the face of the many, many distractions that face the average college student. It might seem at times that our main task is to master the art of holding our liquor, or establishing a name for ourselves within our dorm/fraternity/sorority, or getting the most out of the night life on campus. It's true—college is a time to have fun and experience life on our own—but if we aren't maintaining a good academic standing, none of those things will matter because we'll be packing up and going home. And what about after college? If you want to continue your education, your GPA will influence if and where you can do so. Believe it or not, it can also influence your job opportunities right out of college. I know someone who was actually asked during her first job interview what her GPA was! You will graduate from college with a passing GPA, but just passing may not be good enough, depending on your postgraduate plans. Talk about pressure!

Can you remember a time when learning was fun? For years now you have probably been living in a world where both your future and your sense of who you are—what your abilities and limitations are and how you fit into the "hierarchy" of things—have been determined to a great extent by the grades you've been getting on a report card. If you're someone who gets average grades, you've likely incorporated those grades into your sense of self, as someone who is "average," destined for an average career with an average salary. If you're someone who has struggled with school, consistently or for any period of time, you've likely started to identify with those Ds and Fs as evidence that you're a "loser," destined for failure. And if you're an all-A student, you might find yourself clinging to those grades for a sense of intellectual or personal superiority, as evidence that your life will somehow be better than those with lower grades. At the end of the day, a grade is just a letter on a piece of paper, but the psychological implications for your reality can be enormous. And you are now about to embark on four more years of extreme academic scrutiny.

Before we go any further, I want to remind you that you are *not* your grades. Just like you are not your anger, but the experiencer of anger when someone cuts you off in traffic, you are not your grades, but simply the experiencer of the grades that exist in your reality. As the experiencer, there is no need to personalize your grades. They may have some practical implications, but no matter how big or small those implications, they are *never* a reflection of *who you are*.

Given the amount of weight our society gives grades, you'll probably start to hear, if you haven't already, lots of questions from your family members, friends, and academic advisors, like:

"How are your grades?"

"How did you do on midterms?"

"Are you studying enough?"

"How many credits are you taking?"

"Did you get your paper done yet? How'd you do on it?"

Not only will you be hearing these types of questions from parents and family members, you'll probably be asking yourself the very same questions. Or when you go to bed the night before your final exam, you'll find yourself running through all the "what ifs" in your mind:

"What if I fail?"

"What if I blank out and forget everything I studied?"

"What if my alarm doesn't go off and I miss the exam altogether?"

"What if I my grades are so bad that I have to leave college?"

What you are experiencing here is academic pressure. If you take the "academic" out of the equation, when you get right down to it, you are simply experiencing a state of being of pressure.

Remember, *you* are not the pressure that you experience; you are just the experiencer *experiencing* pressure. Just like any other state of being, you want to start by accepting it.

"I accept that I'm experiencing pressure right now, and that's okay."

Now it's time to apply the four steps:

Know what you don't want.
   "I don't want to fail out of college."

Know what you ultimately want.
   "I want to have a successful academic career. When I do, I will experience success and accomplishment."

Get into the feeling place of your ultimate want.
   "I am willing to consider that I don't need anything in order to experience success and accomplishment right now."

Imagine yourself on stage in your cap and gown, being handed your diploma. Don't wait for this to manifest in your physical reality; experience the state of success and accomplishment right now!

Allow your physical want to come into your experience.
When you experience pressure, doubt, worry, or any state of being that reflects resistance, accept it. Then be willing to consider that you are already having a successful academic experience.

In my junior year of college, to fulfill a requirement I signed up for an economics course. Let's just say, three years out of high school, math was long gone from my head, and I had no idea what to expect going in. I started to experience panic and confusion. Since I was practicing the principles of the Law of Attraction, however, I was aware of what I was experiencing and was able to start to do something about it. As always, I accepted my current state of being: "I accept that I am experiencing panic and confusion right now, and that's okay."

I then identified what I didn't want: "I don't want to fail this class and have to take it over again."

Next I identified what I ultimately wanted: "I want to pass the class, even if it's with a C. When I do, I will experience relief and happiness."

Then I got into the feeling place of my ultimate want: "I'm willing to consider that I don't need anything in order to experience relief and happiness right now." I pictured all of my exams coming back and having at least a C on them.

Next, and most important, I allowed my physical want to come into my experience by accepting the experience of panic and confusion or doubt and anxiety. Then I continued to be willing to consider that I could pass economics with at least a C average.

As you read through my anecdote, you might be thinking to yourselves, "Why did he just ask for a C and not for an A?" Well, it's true, I could have asked for a higher grade, but I'm not sure I was ready to consider that that was a real possibility for me at that point. It's important to start where you are. Why? Because, if you try to convince yourself that you could get an A, but your state of being is actually resistant to that, you end up only expanding resistance. So it's absolutely vital to be realistic about where you are and what you feel, and to build your confidence from there.

Did I pass the course? Indeed I did—with a C! With that success, I gained more confidence, which led me to be willing to consider that I could get Bs on any exam . . . and then As. My overall GPA started to rise as my confidence expanded. That alone felt great!

My friend Andrea went through a similar situation. Here's her story about how she used the Law of Attraction to go from a failing grade to an A in one of her least favorite subjects, chemistry:

> I studied remedial massage in London and started practicing it professionally in health clubs in London and Brisbane. I felt a longing to help people more, so I did a full-time, four-year degree in Bachelor of Health Science in Acupuncture in Brisbane, while working part-time doing telemarketing and remedial massage to help pay for my studies. Part of the curriculum included biochemistry (a subject I had always struggled with). I wasn't looking forward to the experience, considering I averaged just 23 percent in high school chemistry!
>
> The class consisted of about six people, and three or four of the students had failed the course the first time around and were repeating it for the second time. Most people seemed to find this subject difficult. My initial thought was "How am I expected to pass or get a good mark in chemistry, when two-thirds of the class have already failed and are repeating it again? What hope have I got, knowing my past record? I don't want to repeat chemistry for another year!"
>
> I could tell the path I was going down and was sure that I was bound to create my past results, so I decided I needed to look at the situation differently. Instead of worrying myself sick, I decided to change my focus. Instead of asking myself, "How am I ever going to get through this, and what happens if I don't?" I asked myself, "How can I do this, with the most amount of enjoyment and the least amount of stress?"

Instead of resisting them, I loved and accepted as many of my emotions, thoughts, and feelings as I could whenever they came up—for example, "Chemistry is hard and boring," "What happens if I fail again?" At first I didn't believe I could do it, and the self-doubting was pretty constant. But over time, the doubts gradually eased off, and I started to believe and feel inside of me that I could actually pass with an exceptional result, and that chemistry really could be fun and easy for me to learn. I expanded these thoughts even more into my reality, and finally attracted an exam result of 92 percent!!!

Andrea's awareness, willingness to accept what she was experiencing, and willingness to consider that her experience could be different created a reality that reflected what she really wanted!

A grade is a grade, whether you are writing a paper, taking an exam, doing a presentation, or handing in a project. Getting the grade you want is now only four steps away. Your willingness to apply the four steps of deliberate creation and accept all that you're experiencing will create the GPA you want, not the one you "think" you are capable of getting based on self-doubt or a negative past experience.

ATTRACTING A GREAT PROFESSOR

It's common to feel anxious about your new professors, especially if their reputations for assigning brutal readings, pop quizzes, and lengthy term papers precede them. Let me ask you this, though: If you are the creator and you've decided that you are going to create a successful academic career, then does it really matter what professor you get? Since you are creating a successful academic career, it stands to reason that everything in the physical world has to unfold to that end. So, do you *need* to attract a great professor? If you did, then your state of being would be need and we all know what that creates: more opportunities to experience need.

Rather than tell you what kind of professor you should be hoping for, the purpose of this section is to help you see that whatever professor you get, you can work in harmony with that person to achieve what it is you want: academic success.

I know you will probably hear a lot of things from your peers like:

"Professor So-and-so is really hard."

"Professor So-and-so is really boring."

"Make sure you get Professor So-and-so; he's easy."

"Professor So-and-so assigns a lot of reading."

"Professor So-and-so doesn't care if you show up to her class."

And on and on it goes. Remember, if you are an experiencer, then everyone else is an experiencer, too. When you get down to it, everyone is having their own experience, which happens to be unique and particular to them. Why base any decision you make on what someone else says? Their "advice" does not reflect your experience but is specific to their own. Since, as we've seen, you create your own experience and reality, it really shouldn't (or doesn't!) matter what anyone else says. Given this, it doesn't make much sense that another person's experience with a professor should have any ability to determine what your experience will be with that same professor.

Your attention is better placed on your state of being in the moment when it comes to the relationship you have with any of your potential professors. As always, accept whatever you are experiencing, and then:

Know what you don't want.
"I don't want to have a hard time with my professors."

Know what you ultimately want.
"I want to have a harmonious relationship with all my professors; I want to experience harmony."

Get into the feeling place of your ultimate want.
"I am willing to consider that I don't need anything in order to experience harmony right now."
Imagine yourself actually interacting with your professor, not just sitting in the back row of the classroom.

> *Allow your physical want to come into your experience.*
> *When the thought comes in that Professor So-and-so is*
> *anything other than easy to work with, accept the state of*
> *being of doubt and be willing to consider that the professor*
> *might actually be fun and easygoing.*

When it comes to relationships, a lot of the states of being we experience happen while we are in a conversation with someone. Ever had that experience when you are speaking with someone and, because of their tone or the nature of what they're talking about, you can feel yourself starting to get angry? What typically happens? You react out of anger. So what are you creating? Opportunities to experience more anger, which usually result in the other person saying something that makes you even angrier.

With this in mind, pay attention to your state of being when you are speaking with your professors. Are you experiencing fear, confusion, doubt, and insecurity? As you are in the conversation, stay attuned and accept whatever you are experiencing. This may seem hard at first, but give it a try. Don't worry about what is actually being said; you'll take it all in. What's important is that your responses reflect a state of being of acceptance so that the conversation heads in the direction of what you want—a harmonious relationship with your professors!

Of course, you want to pay attention to your state of being during your lectures as well as when you are doing a reading assignment or studying for an exam. If you have the thought, "I hate that Professor So-and-so assigned so much reading," accept that you are experiencing frustration right now and remind yourself that that's okay. Then be willing to consider that you could get the reading done and that you could have a harmonious relationship with a professor that assigns so much reading.

One semester, I took a calligraphy course (a credit is a credit) that people said was taught by a very demanding professor. I have to admit that I let their experiences cause me a bit of fear. I was willing to keep my attention on my experience and not the experience of others and was willing to consider that I could have a great relationship with this professor.

Here's how I started creating: "I accept that I am experiencing fear right now, and that's okay."

Then I identified what I didn't want: "I don't want this class to be a struggle."

Next I identified what I ultimately wanted: "I want a harmonious relationship with my professor."

I then got into the feeling place of my want and became willing to consider that I didn't need anything in order to experience harmony right now. The week before classes started, I repeated in my head "I cannot wait to go to class. I am so excited! Learning calligraphy is going to be a fun and interesting experience."

At this point, I allowed my physical want to come into my experience. When thoughts like "What if they're right? What if this class is a nightmare?" came in, I just accepted that I was experiencing fear and was willing to consider that I could have a harmonious relationship with my professor.

On the first day of class, the first words that came out of my professor's mouth were "This class is not going to be an easy A." I could see the "I knew it" reactions from most of the students in the class. I was willing to accept, however, that I was experiencing doubt and just reminded myself that that was okay. I was willing to consider that I could experience harmony in that very moment. Then, instead of something negative, angry, or fear-based, the positive thoughts starting coming in, like "Wow, she really takes her class seriously; she must really love what she does."

The following Thursday when our class was scheduled to meet again, about 75 percent of the students had dropped out. As the weeks went on, I became friendly with her and vice versa. Because I was experiencing acceptance, I naturally projected positive energy toward her and I received it back in return. I noticed that the students that were clearly experiencing fear didn't connect with her at all. I found myself having one-on-one conversations with her in which I asked her things like how her weekend was and how she got started with calligraphy (not to suck up, but because I was genuinely interested). We ended up having a very harmonious relationship. I ended up getting an A–. The grade was really just a bonus; the real gift for me was realizing that by following the four steps, I could create exactly what I wanted.

CHOOSING A MAJOR

If you thought picking the right college for you was hard, just wait until the time comes to choose a major. There are so many majors to choose from. What if you pick the wrong one? What if you pick one and you fail out of it? What if it doesn't lead to a career you like or are any good at? What if your parents don't approve of the major you choose? There is probably a lot of very real pressure on you to declare your major, so if you are struggling with that, accept that you are experiencing pressure and be willing to consider that whatever major you choose is perfect for you right now.

On a practical level, please keep in mind that just because you have to choose a major by your freshman or sophomore year does not necessarily mean that you have to stick with that major for the rest of your academic experience. One of my closest friends, Dominick, majored in biology. At first he was going to use his biology major to become a radiologist. His reasoning behind going into that field was that radiologists made good money and pursuit of this degree would lead to a lucrative career. Dom's dedication to his studies was truly admirable. I remember the long nights he spent in the library writing papers and the detailed study guides he created for his big exams. I had nothing but respect for his persistence and self-discipline. That said, I couldn't help but notice when he commented, "I cannot wait until I get this over with." When I asked him why, he said he didn't enjoy his major; the material was difficult and it required almost all of his energy and focus.

One semester he took a nutrition course that he loved. Studying for the exams came naturally to him, the course material was more exciting than anything else he had encountered in radiology, and his relationship with his professor was harmonious. Every time he returned from that class, it was like he was on a natural high. He loved telling everyone about the things he learned and how they could incorporate them into their lives.

I remember asking him, "Why not just become a nutritionist?" There was a long pause before he said something along the lines of "Yeah, but I already took all these classes for radiology and I have to go to med school." Talk about resistance! As he was saying this to me, I felt a third person standing between us talking for him. "Should-do Dom" was standing in front of "Want-to-do Dom."

Dom is the type of person who likes to be around people, work in an open environment, and be as far from computers and technology as possible. He loves being outdoors and learning about food. Those two things were very close to his heart. After our conversation, he realized that when he became a radiologist he would be spending most of his time working indoors, glued to a computer screen. This realization definitely raised a red flag for him that he had not paid attention to previously.

After some thought, well into his senior year, Dom made a big decision. He was going to become a nutritionist and skip med school. That not only took a lot of courage, but was also a smart move for his future. Instead of spending years going through med school only to find out that he was not where he wanted to be, he would instead be studying and working in a field he loved.

Dom is a great example of how someone can decide to change his or her major late in the game and still maintain a positive attitude. Dom was not worried. He was not resentful for taking classes that he ultimately did not need to take; he just knew what he wanted to do with his life and went for it. He made it happen and now lives every day of his life doing work he loves!

If you are confused about what major is right for you right now, then apply the four steps to get clear:

"I accept that I am experiencing confusion right now, and that's okay."

Know what you don't want.
"I don't want to be confused about the major I want to declare."

Know what you ultimately want.
"I want to know what major I want to study right now. I ultimately want to experience clarity, relief, happiness, and freedom."

Get into the feeling place of your ultimate want.
Be willing to consider that you don't need anything in order to experience clarity, relief, happiness, and freedom right now.

Allow your physical want to come into your experience. Accept when you are experiencing confusion and be willing to consider that it is possible for you to know what major you want to study. Now when you experience doubt and confusion, you can simply accept and be willing to know again.

Once you decide, accept whatever state of being comes up and you'll be open to making the choices you really want, not the ones you think you have to.

This process will also lead you to take the action of being honest with yourself and others, including those who think you should major in something other than what you really want.

CREDITS

If you are creating a successful college experience, have harmonious relationships with your professors, and are in a major that serves you and truly resonates with your personal experience and aspirations, then credits will naturally take care of themselves.

When you are experiencing acceptance, you will be willing to take actions that support having enough credits to graduate on time. Some of these actions might include:

Making sure you find out the exact number of credits required for graduating college on time.

Laying out the courses you will take each semester based on the requirements of your major.

Mapping out a tentative course schedule for the time you will be attending school.

Meeting with the academic dean or your advisor to introduce yourself and collect any specific information about school credits.

Keeping track of the status of your credits every semester in relation to your tentative four-year course schedule. If it happens that you were unable to take a course in the semester you planned to take it, make that a priority for the next semester.

Keeping a running total of the credits you've earned and matching this total against the total number of credits you need to graduate.

When your attention is on creating the academic experience you really want, managing your credits will seem like a breeze.

Now that you're creating more time for yourself, a strong emotional foundation, and a successful academic experience, let's put some conscious attention on learning how to create the physical results you want.

Chapter 6

THE PHYSICAL RESULTS YOU WANT

The real voyage of discovery consists not in seeking new landscapes but in having new eyes.

—Marcel Proust

By now you're likely getting the hang of the Law of Attraction and starting to see how you can use it as a tool to enhance your college experience: be aware of your current state of being, accept it, and use the four steps of deliberate creation to create what you want (namely, a fun and rewarding academic career). You may be saying, "Got it. What do I do next?" Simple: be aware of your current state of being, accept it, and use the four steps of deliberate creation to create what you want! In other words, using the Law of Attraction is an ongoing, repetitive process. You don't practice the steps once, twice, or even a few times. Like any other skill, it requires commitment, and the more you practice it, the better the principles will work in your college life (and beyond) and the better *you* will ultimately be.

If this should feel daunting (and it's perfectly fine if it does), just remember how simple the steps are. We're not dealing with rocket science here. The steps are easy to practice; they just require the time and willingness on your part to do them. What I'm inviting you to consider at this point is that you are capable of creating profound and powerful life changes. It really is as simple as it sounds (as most powerful things typically are).

In this chapter, we will take a close look at the importance of putting some creative attention on the physical world. Since college is a whole new world for you, you will be expected to deal with issues you may never have had to deal with before like gaining weight, dealing with unwanted roommates or neighbors, taking care of yourself when you are sick, and even making sure you don't run out of toilet paper. Not to worry, though—once you accept and apply the four steps, your experience of this strange, new world can become anything you want it to be!

YOUR BODY

The choices you make at college can take a real toll on your physical body. Binge drinking, pulling all-nighters, and pounding energy drinks can leave you feeling hung over, tired, worn out, and sick. Late-night eating and drinking can lead to the dreaded "freshman fifteen" weight gain, which can easily lead to low self-esteem and worry about your appearance. If you are sick and worried, you won't be able to fulfill your academic responsibilities.

For most of your life, you have probably experienced intense pressure to maintain a standard of physical appearance. Through media, society, family, friends, and high school, you—like most of us—have likely absorbed the notion that you need to look a certain way in order to experience happiness. From what you have learned in this book, however, you know that the state of being of happiness exists inside of you and that you don't need anything to experience it right now. You don't have to look a certain way to experience happiness! As far as your health goes, you have probably been told, both directly and indirectly, that you don't have much control over illness. If you are sick, your only options are to grin and bear it, or see a physician who will prescribe medication to help you feel better.

These are powerful notions, so powerful, in fact, that you are probably thinking that the process of creation will not be of much value in this area of your life. This is simply not true. We are dealing with the principle that you are always expanding opportunities to experience more of your current state of being. It doesn't matter what the physical circumstance is; what matters is your state of being. If you believe that you have no creative control over your physical body, then you are experiencing a state of being of limitation and are therefore expanding opportunities for your physical health to reflect limitation.

What if you could heal yourself of a headache? Cure your case of acne? How about maintain the weight you want without the torture of a diet? What if you could experience energy, vitality, and strength right now? What if you were willing to consider that you actually had creative control over your physical health?

We've already been looking at a process that could help you accomplish all of these things. Whether you are tying to cure yourself of an illness or trying to shed those "freshman fifteen," the process is the same and draws on the fundamentals of the Law of Attraction we've been exploring.

Creating Overall Health

The process of improving your overall health, like everything, begins with acceptance: "I accept that I am experiencing limitation right now, and that's okay."

Know what you don't want.

"I don't want to feel like I have no control over my health."

Know what you ultimately want.

"I want the ability to create the health I want. When I do, I will experience, energy, vitality, beauty, and peace."

Get into the feeling place of your ultimate want.

"I am willing to consider that I don't need anything in order to experience energy, vitality, beauty, and peace right now."

When you start to experience these states of being, you will naturally start to have healthy thoughts and take healthy actions. Picture yourself enjoying the results of those actions. Maybe you start walking more and enjoying the fresh air and you start to notice your pants fit better. Or you start making healthy eating choices, which include drinking fewer energy drinks, and you notice that you are actually experiencing even more energy. You decide not to drink and you see yourself enjoying a relaxing Sunday morning instead of one spent nursing a hangover. Or perhaps you see yourself wide awake and alert in class because you have made it a priority to get more sleep.

Allow your physical want to come into your experience.

When you experience limitation or doubt, accept it and be willing to consider that you don't need anything in order to experience energy, vitality, beauty, and peace right now. Also be willing to consider that it is possible for you to experience the health you want right now!

Losing Weight

There's no secret to losing and maintaining a healthy weight. Pragmatically speaking, the key is to consume fewer calories and exercise your body. Now, we might not be trained nutritionists, but we all basically know what foods are good for us and which ones will tend to tighten our jeans. If we all have this knowledge, why aren't we making the healthy choices that will keep us lean and trim? Because our state of being in relation to our current weight is resistance rather than acceptance. Some among us are looking in the mirror and saying such uplifting things as:

"I need to lose ten pounds."

"I'm so ashamed of how heavy I've gotten."

"I should exercise more."

"I can't believe I ate that donut. I'm so weak."

"How can anyone love me when I'm this fat?"

What typically happens when we say those things? Well, in the face of all this negative self-criticism, we might throw in the towel and give up completely on our health and physical appearance. Or we might decide that enough is enough, start going to the gym, and even deny ourselves that donut. We might do these things for about a week, maybe two, and then we end up right back in front of the mirror saying the same things. Why do we stay in this cycle? Because we haven't addressed the states of being that have been driving our feelings, thoughts, words, and actions all this time. Look at the previous statements. What do they all have in common? They reflect a state of being of need, shame, limitation, weakness, and pressure. If we don't deal with these feelings and confront them head-on, then it doesn't matter what preliminary changes we make—the cycle is bound to continue!

So, using what we know about acceptance and the Law of Attraction, let's start at the beginning: "I accept that I am experiencing need, shame, limitation, weakness, and pressure right now, and that's okay."

Know what you don't want.
"I don't want to be overweight."

Know what you ultimately want.
"I want to drop ten pounds. When I do, I will experience attractiveness, beauty, and confidence."

Get into the feeling place of your ultimate want.
"I'm willing to consider that I don't need anything in order to experience attractiveness, beauty, and confidence right now."
See yourself at your healthy weight, and experience that confidence right now.

Allow your physical want to come into your experience.
Accept when you experience the need, shame, limitation, weakness, and pressure, and be willing to consider that you don't need anything in order to experience attractiveness, beauty, and confidence right now.

Since you are already expanding energy, vitality, beauty, and peace for your overall health and your attention is also on expanding attractiveness and confidence, you will start to notice that your thoughts about how you want to lose the weight will be more in alignment with what you want to do instead of what you *have* to do. If you are doing what you want, don't you think you will continue to do it?

The next thing you know, you will start walking to class more or take the steps instead of the elevator. Maybe your creation partner will create a parking space that requires you to walk a bit more. You'll say no to participating in the midnight pizza run, without feeling like you are denying yourself. You'll notice that you'll want to grab bottled water instead of a soda. Suddenly, that ice cream you used to have after dinner every night becomes a once-a-week treat. You notice you have one, okay, maybe two, instead of four beers at parties now. You feel like you aren't actually *doing* much to lose the weight, but it is coming off anyway. Am I saying don't diet or go to the gym? Nope. But if you choose to, be sure you are aware of your current state of being when you do. If it is limitation ("I have to" or "I should"), then you are only expanding the experience of limitation, which may manifest as not losing any weight.

You may be thinking, "That's all well and good, but I'm still not the weight I want to be." Remember, it's not about the number of pounds you are or aren't; it's about the state of being you ultimately want to experience. You always have the state of being you want to experience inside you right now; you don't have to wait until you lose the ten pounds. In fact, the more you are willing to accept what you are experiencing, the more you are open to experiencing that state of being that will create you losing the ten pounds.

Once I heard a radio show on which the host was recalling a time when she taught a class on the Law of Attraction. One of the men in her group, evidently bald, had said, "No amount of me thinking I'm this, that, or the other thing is going to grow hair on my head." The host asked him to describe how his experience would be different if he did have hair. I paraphrase here, but he went on to say that he would be more confident, attractive, and assertive. The host said that, as the man was talking about the experience, he got up and started walking around the room. He looked the other participants in the eye as he spoke. His voice was strong. After he was done, he sat down and the host asked the women in the room what they thought about him. All of them said that at first they didn't think much about him, but when he was describing what he would experience, they thought that he was attractive and confident. He didn't need hair to experience what he wanted; he simply had to be willing to drop the need for the hair to experience what he ultimately wanted!

Okay, one last time: It's not the physical thing you want; it's the state of being you think you are going to experience when you have that thing. You don't have to lose weight to experience any state of being right now, and when you are willing to experience that state of being right now, you will naturally take the actions in the physical world to obtain the physical thing you want.

Creating Health When You Are Experiencing Illness

Where do you want to be when you are feeling sick? Like most of us, probably at home, in bed, with someone taking care of you, making you chicken noodle soup, bringing you tissues and cough drops, and telling you it's all going to be okay. Now you find yourself in a dorm room, alone. You realize that you have to get up and make yourself the soup, go to the drug store to get those tissues, and, on top of it all, be the one to assure yourself that it's all going to be okay (when, in all honesty, you're not so sure that it will be).

What states of being do you experience when you are experiencing illness? Well, for starters, weakness, lack, limitation, fear, and even loneliness. Let's go through the steps:

"I accept that I'm experiencing weakness, lack, limitation, fear, and loneliness right now, and that's okay."

Know what you don't want.
"I don't want to feel yucky anymore!"

Know what you ultimately want.
"I want to feel better. When I do, I will experience energy, strength, and happiness."

Get into the feeling place of your ultimate want.
Be willing to consider that you don't need anything in order to experience energy, strength, and happiness right now. Feel those states of being and let them expand.

Allow your physical want to come into your experience.
When you experience weakness, lack, limitation, fear, and loneliness, accept it and be willing to consider that you could be well right now.

Sometimes you may not be experiencing full-on sickness; maybe you're just experiencing a muscle ache, for example. I can't tell you the number of times I have felt an ache and it disappeared when I simply accepted that I was experiencing limitation. The same is true with headaches. We can't focus on two things simultaneously. When my attention is on the state of being, it is off the physical pain. Since I am dealing with the cause of the ache, the state of being of limitation, it's not long before the headache is simply gone. Give this a try and see for yourself!

When you are in a state of being of acceptance, you will know how you want to go about physically treating your illness as well. Be sure to seek support and advice when you want it, though.

Once you are on track with creating your overall health and maintaining your weight, you'll start to notice that you don't get sick as much anymore. Since you are now expanding what you want—great health—your physical body will start reflecting it!

Still doubting that you have creative power over your physical body? Take a deep breath, accept that you're experiencing doubt right now, and take a few minutes to read Krissy's story:

> Going into the doctor's office, I knew something was deeply wrong. It was that sixth sense we all have about ourselves; I just did not realize how bad things were. Leukemia was my diagnosis—stage 3. They had caught it, but not before it had begun to spread. Here I was, in my early twenties, sitting in this stuffy office, in this uncomfortable chair, staring at a doctor who was telling me I was going to die. Oh, they were going to try and do everything, but he let it be known that I needed to put my affairs in order, as he did not hold out much hope that I would make it until the end of the year. Next to me my parents were crying, but I was just numb. How do you begin to grasp the thought that this is truly it? I remember walking out of the office, getting looks from the nurses that said it all—"You poor thing, you are going to die."
>
> Once outside I was hit with a cold blast of February air. It was snowing, and I remember thinking, "My God, it's so beautiful." The snow was blanketing everything in shimmering white, it was all so pure and so serene, and I knew: *This was not it for me.* I was not going without a fight. Something had awakened within me. I turned around and marched right back inside, passing the nurses, not stopping

when asked what I was doing. I walked right back into that doctor's office, looked him square in the eyes, and let him know that I was not ready, that I was not giving up hope, that I was going to fight, and that he better change his attitude as well. I had come too far, had been on the brink of death before and come back, and I would come back again. My whole future was ahead of me, I had things I needed to accomplish. I had yet to truly make a difference and I had not yet made my mark on the world. I told him that it was time to prepare a battle plan, because together we were going to fight this thing. It has been a long and painful year, but it has been a year of triumph, both mentally and physically. The cancer is gone, and I am well on my way to a complete recovery!

It may seem that Krissy was in a state of being of resistance when she decided to "fight" for her life. But she was really experiencing a state of being of the acceptance of the fear she was experiencing. In a state of being of acceptance, she was open to seeing the beauty that surrounded her. That then expanded into the experience of determination that she was going to change her physical reality. Because she was in acceptance, her thoughts reflected positive ideas on how she was going to beat her illness, and she did. Know this: You have the same power! The next time you find yourself holed up in your dorm room, nursing a cold, worrying about what classes you might miss as a consequence and how you're ever going to make up all your lost work, know that you are only four steps away from feeling better and getting easily back on track!

YOUR DORM

So, it's time for dorm room selection, and you want that perfect single on the corner with the quad view or that suite that you can share with six of your friends. You're excited about the prospects for a new living situation, feeling positive about the opportunities that await you, but then the thought creeps in, "What if someone else takes it first?" Once that thought gets in there, it takes on a life of its own. Before you know it, you've completely convinced yourself that there's no way you're going to get that single, and that spot in the suite is as good as someone else's.

When that thought comes in, you know what to do next:

"I accept that I am experiencing doubt right now, and that's okay."

Know what you don't want.
 "I don't want to end up in a dorm room I don't want."

Know what you ultimately want.
 "I want the dorm room I want. When I get it, I will experience happiness and contentment."

Get into the feeling place of your ultimate want.
 "I'm willing to consider that I don't need anything in order to experience happiness and contentment right now."
 Experience them now and see yourself being handed the keys to the room you want.

Allow your physical want to come into your experience.
 When you experience doubt again, be willing to accept it and experience happiness and contentment.

I know that it might seem really important to get the exact dorm room you want for academic or social reasons (or both). Keep in mind, however, that you are the creator of your experience, so even if you don't end up with the exact dorm room you want, you are still creating opportunities to experience more happiness and contentment in your life. Maybe your creation partner puts you in the dorm room that just happens to be right next to your future boyfriend or girlfriend. If you don't get exactly the physical thing you want, accept that you are experiencing disappointment and be willing to consider that your creation partner is still delivering all that you ultimately want and more.

Once you are in your dorm room, you might find that you have landed next to insensitive, loud neighbors like I did my sophomore year, when I moved in beside two girls who liked to play their music . . . and liked to play it *loud*. It was so loud, in fact, that I could hear their tunes blaring even over my own headphones. I tried everything: a pillow over the head, fingers in my ears, and going to the library to study. Some nights when there was no music on, I would lie there in a state of anticipation, just waiting for it to come on—and it did, without fail. At some point, I realized that the reason nothing I did to improve or change the situation worked was because I was reacting, not creating.

So I accepted that I was experiencing frustration and anger and determined that that was okay.

I decided I *didn't want* to be kept up by loud music anymore.

I decided that I *ultimately wanted* to study in silence and sleep in a peaceful environment. I knew when this happened that I would be experiencing peace and happiness.

I was *willing* to know that I didn't need anything in order to experience peace and happiness right then and there.

Then, when I experienced anger and frustration, I accepted those states of being and became willing to consider that I could study and rest in peace.

Once I was in a state of being of acceptance, I noticed my thoughts started to change. I decided to put more attention on what I really wanted. With that, I decided that instead of dwelling on my frustration and negativity, I was going to be positive about the situation and write down everything I loved about the music.

The first thing I put on paper was my gratitude that I could hear at all—what a gift to be able to hear the complex rhythms and melodies of music (even if it wasn't music of my own choosing). Then I started thinking about the two girls. I wrote down that they were always nice to me and that they always made an effort to say hello to me in the hallway. One of them even slipped a few stickers under my door just to be nice. I also told myself that I was happy that I had my own place to stay that was away from home, and that I was happy and grateful that I could even go to college in the first place.

Well, within a few days one of the girls decided to transfer. She packed her stuff and left within two weeks from the day I wrote down all that stuff. After she moved, I never heard the music again.

The remaining roommate wound up hanging out at her friend's room 24/7 and just came to her room to sleep and pick up some books. How amazing is that? I still thank my creation partner to this day for the physical results it created for me.

Another way to approach your neighbors is by remembering that you are in a relationship with them. Since you create, you have the power to create any relationship with them. So, what kind of relationship do you want to have with your neighbors, or your own roommate, for that matter?

Know what you don't want.

"I don't want to have a hard time with my roommate or neighbors."

Know what you ultimately want.

"I want to have a harmonious relationship with everyone around me. I want to experience harmony."

Get into the feeling place of your ultimate want.

"I am willing to consider that I don't need anything in order to experience harmony right now."

Get into the feeling place of working with, not against, your roommate and neighbors. See yourself happily interacting with these people. Maybe you're spending a little time together laughing or sharing some of your macaroni and cheese or microwavable popcorn.

Allow your physical want to come into your experience.

When the thought comes in that your roommate or neighbor is anything other than easy to work with and be around, accept the state of being of doubt and be willing to consider that they could be.

Remember what we said about your relationship with your professors. It's the same thing here. The relationship you have is determined completely by you. It's about your state of being. So be aware of what state of being you experience when you think or speak about your roommate or neighbor. *Accept* whatever it is that you are experiencing so that your next thoughts, words, and actions reflect harmony. Simply stated, if you are experiencing anger, you will react out of anger, which will only expand anger! So, practice acceptance and see how it is possible to work in harmony with someone you initially thought you could never work with at all.

YOUR BASIC NEEDS

When I lived at home with my parents, I never needed to think about buying toilet paper, soap, and groceries for myself. That was always taken care of for me. But when I moved out, those basic needs became my responsibility. Suddenly, my needs took over my wants. I needed cleaning supplies to clean my bathroom, but I wanted that new iPod so I could enjoy my play list of ten thousand songs. Having to decide between a need and a want becomes frustrating because if I go with the need, then I experience resentment because I didn't get my want. And if I go with the want, then I experience stress because the need doesn't get taken care of.

Once I accepted that I was experiencing frustration, I was willing to consider something new, which was that all of my basic needs are taken care of easily.

Go ahead and say it yourself: "All of my basic needs are taken care of easily." When I said it, it felt really good! I did have to accept when I experienced doubt, but I started to notice that I no longer worried about my basic needs, I just took care of them. Without all the worry, I was free to put more attention on my *wants*.

If you find yourself worrying about how you will stock your ramen noodle collection or keep shampoo in the shower, accept that you are experiencing worry right now and remember that that's okay. Then be willing to consider that all of your needs are taken care of easily. Remember, the more you focus on the lack of something, the more lack of that something you get in return. So accept and be willing to consider, and see how easy it is for you to take care of your basic needs.

Money

If there is one thing that seems like it is always in short supply, it's money. You don't have to be in college to experience this one. Many adults, too, struggle with lack of money, but you are in a unique position. You have been placed in an environment with a lot of academic, emotional, and physical demands that you suddenly have to face and, on top of that, you also now have very real financial demands. Unlike adults who have had lots of practice handling their money and who take in a steady income, this is likely the first time in your life that you've had to be fiscally responsible and, because you're not getting paid to go to college, the amount of money you have to work with probably feels meager (at best).

Your basic needs, tuition, books, social activities, and travel to and from campus (not to mention your trips to and from home) all add up to a big pile of money. I would always see my friends stressing out about buying books, going out with friends, paying for loans, and dealing with the expenses of living on their own. Some students even got stressed that their parents had to buy things for them.

Do you hear yourself saying things like:

"I can't afford this."

"I don't have enough money."

"I'm completely broke."

"I wish I could, but I just don't have the funds."

"I would never pay that much for that."

"Who could afford that?"

"I'll never be able to pay off my loans."

If you do, then you are probably experiencing a ton of resistance around money.

Here's a test (and you thought there weren't going to be any tests! Not to worry, there's only one question and by now it should be a no-brainer for you):

What creates opportunities to experience wealth?

Let me make it even easier by making it multiple choice:

What creates opportunities to experience more wealth?

A. Money

B. Luck

C. The state of being of wealth, prosperity, and abundance

D. Winning the lottery

The answer, of course, is C: "The state of being of wealth, prosperity, and abundance." You've heard it before, "The rich get richer while the poor get poorer." Why is that? Because the wealthy are experiencing a state of being of wealth and the poor are experiencing a state of being of scarcity!

What are you experiencing? More to the point, what do you want to experience?

"I accept that I am experiencing lack right now, and that's okay."

Know what you don't want.

"I don't want to experience lack of money ever."

Know what you ultimately want.

"I want to experience having more than enough money. When I have it, I will experience wealth, security, and happiness."

Get into the feeling place of your ultimate want.

Be willing to consider that you don't need anything in order to experience wealth, security, and happiness right now. Go ahead, experience it right now!

Allow your physical want to come into your experience.

Accept when you experience lack and scarcity. Be willing to experience wealth, security, and happiness right now!

When you do, you'll hear yourself saying things like:

"I have more than enough money to buy that."

"I am going out with my friends and treating them all to dessert."

"My bank account is growing and growing each month! I love it."

"I can afford all my basic needs and my wants!"

"I have more than enough money to donate to a cause I love."

"I know my loans will be paid in full!"

The person who is in a state of acceptance and experiencing the state of being of wealth is the person who comes up with ideas on how to expand their physical wealth. Sometimes your creation partner will even surprise you with unexpected income.

So, pay attention and don't forget your creation partner is always working for you. Sometimes we can't see beyond physical reality, but our creation partner can. Sometimes what happens seems like a miracle. But there are no miracles, just opportunities to experience more of your current state of being.

I have one more suggestion on money. Remember when we were talking about time and how we usually experience lack when we think about it? I invited you to accept the experience of lack and to be willing to consider that you had more than enough time. Well, I now invite you to try this out with money. When your thought is "I don't have enough money," accept that you are experiencing lack and that that's okay. Be willing to consider that you could have more than enough money. Doesn't that feel good? You are just opening yourself up to a new possibility. Think about it: as it stands, the only possibility you are open to now is that you don't and therefore won't have enough money. Isn't that your experience? Isn't it worth being willing to consider that you could have more than enough money?

MOVING ON NOW

Wow, we have addressed a lot so far. Now it's time for some fun by learning how to create the social world you want.

Chapter 7

THE SOCIAL RESULTS YOU WANT

The reason I don't drink is that I want to know when I'm having a good time.

—Nancy Astor

I t's your first day at college. Your parents just left. You are unpacking and making small talk with your new roommate. You're thinking about your bedroom at home and wondering how everything you brought to college is going to fit in less than half the size of what you're used to. As you're making idle chitchat with this new person you're going to have to share a space with, you start to think about your friends from high school. Your roommate interrupts your chain of thought to tell you that she's off to her boyfriend's room (they were lucky enough to get into the same college), where, she informs you, she will be spending most of her time. A couple of weeks ago you were surrounded by your friends and family. You felt supported and sure of yourself in their company. Now you're standing in an empty dorm room and that's when it really hits you: "I'm way out of my element here."

You leave high school at the top of the social rung. When you get to college, you realize you're back at the bottom and, worse yet, you're pretty much on your own. Talk about fear and anxiety! It may seem like it will be impossible for you to meet people you can really connect with, but trust me, it isn't as hard as your current states of being of fear and doubt may be telling you it is. With everything you've gathered from reading this book, you likely realize at this point that you have a choice about how you approach the challenges in front of you, particularly those relating to developing new relationships. You can create a transition that is both easy and enjoyable or you can choose one that is hard and stressful.

CREATING YOUR SOCIAL LIFE

You know that creating something new has to start with accepting your current state of being about what already is. Right now, when it comes to your social life, you are probably experiencing states of being of fear, loneliness, loss, insecurity, and need. Accept these as you experience them:

"I accept that I'm experiencing fear right now, and that's okay."

"I accept that I'm experiencing loneliness right now, and that's okay."

"I accept that I'm experiencing insecurity right now, and that's okay."

"I accept that I'm experiencing need right now, and that's okay."

Once you accept these experiences, it's important to pay attention to what assumptions you are making, or what negative ideas and attitudes are affecting your states of being, and be willing to challenge them.

Here are a few examples:

"I'll never make friends" becomes *"I'm willing to consider that I could make new friends."*

"I won't have time for friends" becomes *"I'm willing to consider that I'll have plenty of time for friends."*

"It will be hard to make friends" becomes *"I'm willing to consider that it could be easy to make friends."*

"I have nothing in common with the people I've met so far" becomes *"I'm willing to consider that I could have things in common with lots of people at my school."*

If you are feeling limited in your new relationships, pay attention to the state of being you are experiencing and allow yourself to consider something new. This will open you up to creating new possibilities.

Now that you are open, use the four steps of deliberate creation to identify and create the social experience you really want:

Know what you don't want.
"I don't want to go through this college experience alone."

Know what you ultimately want.
"I want to have lots of strong friendships, and do lots of fun things while I'm at college. When I do, I will experience happiness, connectedness, security, and fulfillment."

Get into the feeling place of your ultimate want.
Be willing to consider that you don't need anything to experience happiness, connectedness, security, and fulfillment right now. Start to experience these states of being right now. See how good they feel?

Allow your physical want to come into your experience.
Be aware and accept when fear, loneliness, insecurity, and need come up. Continue to be willing to consider that it is possible for you to experience strong friendships and a fulfilling social life at college.

Before we move on, I would like to address a very important point about the state of being of need when it comes to relationships. When you are experiencing a state of being of need, what you are saying is that you need something outside of you in order to experience a state of being that is already inside of you right now. In other words, "I need friends in order to experience happiness." You are tying your happiness to something, or *someone* in this case. Since you think your happiness is the person, you will fear losing them. Now the state of being of fear will expand in addition to the state of being of need. Because they are expanding, you will start to have thoughts, say words, and take actions that reflect need and fear. You know deep down inside that things aren't really what you want, but you just can't help yourself because you are now so afraid of losing the happiness that is now embodied by your friend.

If you need a relationship in order to experience happiness, when you actually get a relationship, you are still expanding need, so the relationship will never measure up to what you want it to be because you are going to need it to be more. If you are experiencing need, it's not possible for you to experience fulfillment. Since you are not getting what you think you need, you will start to resent the other person for not being enough. Or you will feel like you aren't enough. In either case, you will just be expanding the feeling of need and creating opportunities to feel frustration and resentment. Ugh!

Bottom line: need is a relationship killer! The more you need someone, the less you are able to really love that person. Love is freedom; need is restriction. It's impossible to experience them at the same time. Think about relationships you've been in or ones you've witnessed firsthand. What happens to the relationships that start from a place of need? They typically can't sustain themselves for very long and die after a time that is marked by jealousy, envy, frustration, anger, and mistrust. No one is having fun. How could that be love?

Because they are new and are not weighted with emotional routines as some of your older friendships may be, the relationships you make while at the beginning of college will give you a good opportunity to practice what we've been talking about. Pay attention to your state of being at the beginning stages of the relationship. If you do what I invited you to do, you will be well on your way to creating friendships and partnerships that you truly want, not ones that you need. As your relationships grow, pay attention to your state of being and accept what you're experiencing. If things aren't going well in a relationship, the temptation may be to blame the other person, but, as should be clear at this point, your experience of any relationship has nothing to do with anyone else, but with your own state of being. Just be aware and accept what you are experiencing so that you remain open to experiencing what you want in all of your relationships.

The independence you are going to experience in college is really exciting. But with that independence come a lot more opportunities to make important decisions, especially when it comes to your social experience. We will get into more detail as we go through this chapter, but I encourage you to keep in mind what I mentioned about need. If you are experiencing need, you are bound to make choices that lead to actions you might end up regretting. If you do, be sure to accept that you are experiencing regret, embarrassment, guilt, or even self-loathing. By accepting what you are experiencing, you will learn from what you've done and move on. Peer pressure only exists because of the state of being of need. If you were experiencing fulfillment, there would be no reason for you to experience pressure to do anything.

Okay, so back to creating your overall experience. You've decided that you want to have lots of friends and fun. You are willing to experience happiness, connectedness, security, and fulfillment.

Now think about ways that you want to meet people. Maybe you'll join a student group, or work at the campus press, or you'll meet people at the gym playing intramural sports. Since you are not in need, you won't feel that you "have to" join that fraternity and do things you don't want to do because it's the only way you'll meet people.

When you are experiencing acceptance, your attention is on the excitement of meeting new people and doing what you enjoy, instead of on the dread that comes with the thought that you'll never meet people. Congratulations! You are now well on your way to creating strong relationships and a fulfilling social college experience.

FRIENDS FROM HOME

As you start to make friends at college, you may find that friendships from home become strained. This makes a lot of sense and is perfectly natural, because you and your friends are all experiencing a huge life change. Because you are no longer together, you may start to wonder if location was the main reason you spent time with these folks. You may start to experience frustration because you feel that you are no longer connected with your old friends, and they may experience jealousy because you don't call as much anymore.

Not to worry, this is all normal stuff! The best we can do during these times of transition is to accept what we're experiencing and be honest with all those involved. You may experience guilt because you would rather spend time with your new college friends. Or maybe you're the one experiencing jealousy because your best friend from high school doesn't seem to pick up the phone and check in as often anymore. Or maybe you left a girlfriend behind and are experiencing resentment because you're still tied to the relationship and yet you want the freedom to date. Accept these states of being! They are all okay. When you do, I invite you to be willing to consider that the best thing you can do is *be honest* about how you're feeling. I know sometimes we think it is important to spare people's feelings, so we resist expressing to them our true thoughts and feelings, which is really just lying by omission.

From a state of being of acceptance, you can be honest and tell those you care about what you are experiencing and why you want what you want. And, in a place of acceptance, you'll likewise want to give others a chance to tell you what they really want. If your wants are in alignment, then you can decide how you are going to move forward. If they're not? Then you can both move forward in different directions, with honesty and grace. This may be painful at first, but if you accept that you're experiencing pain and remind yourself that that's okay, you'll move through whatever pain exists, and both you and the person you were honest with will be better for it.

Try to remember that love is energy and that energy never dies. When two people decide to end a relationship—whether it's romantic or friendly in nature—it's the relationship that changes, not the love. I personally find that very comforting to know that the end of a friendship or romantic relationship does not mean that two people don't love each other anymore. In essence, their honesty proves how much they really love each other.

TO DATE OR NOT TO DATE

Dating can be fun or it can be a real drag. Which do you want it to be? Do you really want to believe it is a drag, or are you willing to consider that dating can be fun? Do you want to believe that there are no available partners out there, or are you willing to consider that there are plenty of wonderful people available for you to date?

I think there is a real opportunity to take the emphasis off dating and put it on creating the partnership you want. If the relationship is based on mutual appreciation and not need, then having a girlfriend or boyfriend during this time can be a real bonus. Simply do the four steps of deliberate creation, go about experiencing the states of being you want right now, and then let your creation partner orchestrate how you meet your new partner.

As always, accept what you're experiencing. Maybe it's lack—you wish you had a partner. Or maybe it's limitation—you don't think you'll ever find the right partner. Or maybe it's need—you feel that you need a partner in order to feel loved. Or perhaps insecurity—you need a partner in order to survive college. Go ahead and accept whatever it is that you're experiencing right now.

Next, it's time to practice those steps again:

Know what you don't want.
"I don't want my partnership to monopolize my time."

Know what you ultimately want.
"I want a partner who loves me for who I am. I want a partnership where we both love our lives and are willing to balance both our worlds. When I am in this partnership, I will experience love, connectedness, support, fun, and security."

Get into the feeling place of your ultimate want.
Be willing to consider that you don't need anything in order to experience love, connectedness, support, fun, and security right now.

Allow your physical want to come into your experience.
Accept when you experience any state of being that is the opposite of love, connectedness, support, fun, and security. Then be willing to know that your partner is out there and is coming in your direction!

If you want to date and not get involved in a relationship, you can follow the same process and create your dating experience. As always, be sure to pay attention to your state of being and accept whatever it is while you're dating. That way you will be sure to be honest, which will save you a lot of stress and worry when you decide to end a dating relationship with someone.

If you are experiencing acceptance and not need, you will be better able to decide if you want to have a sexual relationship with your partner or the person you're dating. Remember, having sex is your choice. If you are experiencing pressure from a partner or a date, accept that you are experiencing pressure and then be willing to know if this is the step you want to take with this person. Once you accept that you are experiencing pressure, your honest answer to that question will bubble up and you'll be willing to share it with the other person involved. If someone is saying that they need sex with you for any reason, then they are coming from a state of being of need. If they are, you'll want to ask yourself if you want to have any type of relationship with someone who thinks they need you.

I have to say it again: honesty with yourself first and then others is the most important thing you can do to ensure that you experience what you want, even when it scares you. So be sure to accept, get honest, and then act accordingly.

STAYING IN OR COMING OUT

You may get to college and start to question your sexuality. When it comes to public acceptance, coming out these days is a lot easier than it's ever been. When it comes to self or family acceptance, however, coming out can still be an extremely difficult process. The states of being around this topic can be fear, doubt, worry, confusion, and self-loathing (to name just a few). If you are going through this process, accept these feelings as they come up. Be willing to understand what you want. Know that you don't have to declare yourself as anything—gay, straight, or bisexual. Be willing to consider that being honest with yourself is the best thing to do. Then be willing to consider that being honest with everyone else is ultimately the best thing to do as well.

As you accept, you will experience the courage and strength to make the choices and take actions that reflect what you want. If you decide that you want to start sharing with people your feelings and thoughts about your sexuality, I invite you to start with the people you know will give you unconditional support. If there is no one in your life you feel loves you unconditionally, then seek help on campus. Today there are gay, lesbian, bi, and transgender organizations right on campus that can guide and support you. Continue to practice acceptance as you get the support you want and see where that takes you. Your willingness to be authentic with yourself is very powerful and will open you up to a whole new world!

DRINKING AND DRUGS

Drinking and drug use at college are a reality. Here are some sobering statistics: According to the Core Institute, an organization that surveys college drinking practices, the average male freshman consumes 7.39 drinks per week and the female 3.86 per week. The academic impact of this amount of drinking is that 31 percent of college students missed a class and 22 percent failed an exam or essay. In addition, some 159,000 of the nation's current freshmen will drop out of school because of alcohol and drug use. The survey was conducted in 2005 and sampled 33,379 undergrads on fifty-three U.S. campuses.

If you are consciously creating the emotional, academic, physical, and social experience you want, are accepting whatever states of being that aren't in alignment with what you want, and are willing to consider that you can have all that you want, there would be no real reason for you to get hammered every Thursday, Friday, and Saturday night during your college experience. Drinking excessively and taking drugs are actions that stem from states of being of fear, insecurity, doubt, confusion, panic, and need.

If you notice that you are choosing to drink or take drugs, you want to take a step back and ask yourself, "What state of being am I experiencing right now?" Accept whatever state of being it is and then choose what you want to do. Maybe you'll choose to drink, but you'll end up only having one or two before you call it quits. If you are staying conscious and accepting between opportunities to drink, when the choice comes up again, maybe next time you will pass.

Going to parties and having fun is all part of the college experience. These times can be enjoyed, but can result in a "morning after" that we simply don't want to face. This is where you want to be very aware of your state of being. Besides an awful hangover, you may be experiencing embarrassment, self-loathing, judgment, guilt, sadness, regret, shame, insecurity, panic, and so on. Whatever you do, just accept any or all of these states of being. What happens if you don't? It's very likely that you will push them down, they'll continue to expand, and then you'll make the choice to drink more to numb the pain that these states of being expand into! This is where the cycle of resistance begins and continues to expand until you become aware and accept.

If you are gentle with yourself and accept whatever state of being comes up, you will then know what you want to do next. Maybe there are some apologies you'll want to make. Maybe it's time to be honest with someone about what you really want next. Maybe you'll be honest with yourself that college isn't right for you and now you'll have the confidence to tell your parents, and start creating a life for yourself that is right for you. Whatever the real issue is, you won't be able to deal with it if you are experiencing a state of being of resistance.

Drinking and taking drugs are symptoms of a state of being; the state of being you are experiencing is the cause. Once you start dealing with the cause, the symptom will no longer exist. You'll be on track to deal with the real issue and you will be better able to deal with it because you are now dealing with it in a state of being of acceptance, not resistance.

If you are already drinking excessively or taking drugs consistently, then you might be experiencing some level of addiction. Remember, as the experiencer, you are not the addiction nor all the not-so-wonderful stuff that comes along with it. You are the experiencer experiencing a state of being of addiction. This state of being of addiction has manifested into a physical addiction for which you will ultimately want to seek professional help. But first, a state of being is a state of being, so just accept it: "I accept that I'm experiencing addiction right now, and that's okay." Now ask yourself, "What do I want to do about it?" Maybe you'll share your thoughts and feelings with a friend (be sure the friend you share your concerns with isn't one who also shares your addiction). You'll want to get professional help to deal with the physical addiction that has manifested. Seek this help wherever you feel is right for you. Maybe you'll want to go home and get support there. Maybe you'll want to stay at college and work on it. Either way, help and support will be very important for you to move forward, so take full advantage of them.

Doreen, the coauthor of this book, shared her college drinking experience with me. I think it gives a clear demonstration of how resistance builds and ends up exploding when we aren't aware:

> I didn't really drink a lot in high school, but when I did, I tended to get really drunk. Looking back now, I can see that even though I was an athlete, popular, and had a

lot of fun, I was still unhappy. I always felt like I wasn't enough, and didn't do enough. On top of that, I was starting to question my sexuality, so you can throw self-loathing into the mix, too.

Of course I thought a change of scenery would solve all the turmoil inside me, but as I learned very quickly, "Wherever you go, there you are." So by the time I got to college, I was experiencing denial, which expanded into full-on insecurity and need. I needed friends, I needed my mother to like me, I needed someone to know that I was unhappy, and I didn't know what to do about it. I needed to make sure no one knew my secret. Instead of seeking support, I resisted all these feelings and did what I thought I should do to make friends: I partied.

You know me: I was the unhappy, angry drunk you see at parties. Or I was the happy-go-lucky drunk that would be happy to make sure you got home safely. Or sometimes I was the exuberant, loud drunk in your hallway keeping you up late at night. I was the one who passed out and blacked out. I was the one who hooked up with people because I felt I had to in order to experience any form of connectedness.

One particularly embarrassing night, I passed out in the girls' bathroom. At this stage, I thought for sure that all my friends had abandoned me, but one friend did come down to my room to check up on me. I didn't ask her how I ended up in the bathroom, or eventually in bed. I asked her if she thought I was an alcoholic. She said she didn't think I was an alcoholic, what she thought was that I was really unhappy. I agreed.

I wish I could tell you that after our conversation I magically transformed my life, but I didn't. I continued to experience unhappiness because I didn't know that the best thing I could do was accept that I was experiencing unhappiness and that that would eventually open me up to happiness. What I did do was try to be honest with myself, but I was still experiencing need and self-loathing. I thought that when I got the grades I wanted, I would be happy. Or when I came out, all my problems would be solved and I would be loved. Or that when college was over, I could just leave all the fear, confusion, and doubt behind. I did get the grades, I did come out, and I did graduate college, but I was still unhappy, unfulfilled, fearful, confused, and full of doubt.

Had I known then what I know now, twenty years later, I could have created in a whole different direction and avoided lots of heartache and struggle. What I know now is that happiness was always there, available to me. The illusion was that I needed anything outside of me to experience it. This need led to much too much suffering. The suffering is over for me now, and it can be for you too!

No matter how embarrassed and scared you are, you can change the course you're on. Be patient and gentle with yourself as you accept what you are experiencing and you will begin to really know that you do have the power to create your new course!

It doesn't matter when you choose to start consciously creating your college social experience. Even if you have only one semester left, you can make it what you really want it to be, not what you think it has to be!

P.S. A QUICK EXERCISE TO EXPERIENCE CONNECTION

Here's a quick exercise if you find yourself longing to experience connection.

Accept that you are experiencing disconnection right now, and that's okay.

Be willing to consider that you don't need anything in order to experience connection right now.

Now, make eye contact with everyone you encounter. That means everyone. The person you pass in the street. Your professor. The most popular person on campus. Your worst enemy. Everyone!

Disconnection manifests in insecurity, which leads to lack of contact with others. Once you accept the experience of disconnection, you are open to connection with others, and the most intimate of connections is direct eye contact. Once you start connecting, you will be amazed at how quickly you realize that you could never actually be disconnected from anyone. You've always been connected; you've just been experiencing disconnection!

Chapter 8

LET'S REVIEW

*If you think you can do
a thing, or think you can't
do a thing, you're right.*

—Henry Ford

We've covered a lot of territory in this book. You've learned that:

There is a universal law called the Law of Attraction that can be simply defined as "like attracts like."

You are always creating your reality, all of it!

You are not your experiences; you are the experiencer of them.

As the experiencer, you are always experiencing states of being.

States of being are always expanding and are the cause of your feelings, thoughts, words, and actions, as well as your perception of your physical reality.

As the experiencer, you are always creating opportunities to experience more of your current state of being.

You are not alone; you have a creation partner that takes care of the "how" of how physical things come into your experience.

You are free to experience any state of being at any time.

When you are aware of your current state of being, you have the power to consciously create.

The state of being of resistance expands whatever state of being you are resisting.

Your opportunity is to accept your current state of being so that you are open and free to choose a new experience.

You can be willing to consider anything, and that willingness opens you up to new possibilities!

Once you accept your current state of being, you can deliberately create by using the four steps of deliberate creation:

1. Know what you don't want.

2. Know what you ultimately want, that is, the state of being

you are going to experience when you have the physical thing you want.

3. Get into the feeling place of your ultimate want. Be willing to consider that you don't need anything in order to experience the state of being you want right now.

4. Allow your physical want to come into your experience. Be aware and accept your current state of being, no matter what it is. Then be willing to know that you can have what you truly want.

You can apply these concepts and this process to create the emotional, academic, physical, and social results that you want at college.

Finally, I want you to understand that what you've learned can be consciously applied for the rest of your life! You are always creating. The question is: Are you always creating in the direction you really want? You will be if you are willing to be aware and accept. This is your power in creating the life you really want!

STAYING IN TOUCH

There is no need for you to take this journey alone. Check out www.positivefeelingsrule.com to find other like-minded individuals, who are also learning to apply the principles of the Law of Attraction to their experiences, in college and beyond. Take a second to check out what others have to say about the process, or should you feel so inclined at any point, feel free to share your own experiences with this material and/or ask any questions about how you can practically apply what you've learned in this book.

CREATE AWAY

You have the knowledge, the four steps of deliberate creation, and examples of how you can practically apply what you've learned to create the college experience you really want. Now all you need is the willingness to put it into practice. When you choose to, you will see that the emotional, academic, physical, and social experiences you really want have never been, and never will be, more than four steps away!

LIFE JOURNEY PLAN

One of the great things that has helped me accomplish my goals in life has been what I call a "Life Journey Plan." It was something I created to help me stay on track with what I wanted to create in my life. I have passed this plan to most of my friends and they love it. This is something you may want to try when you are experiencing acceptance and possibility.

The plan consists of four parts:

1. Positive things in your life

2. Achievements

3. Short-term goals

4. Long-term goals

Here is the breakdown on what each means:

Positive things in your life are things that you give thanks to. They can be people, material things, or intangible things. Example: A loving parent, a beautiful car, a wonderful job, and a healthy body are all examples of positive things to be grateful for.

Achievements are things that you have already accomplished. Example: "I aced my statistics final."

Short-term goals are things that you would like to accomplish in the near future—in a day, a week, or a month's time. Example: "I want to ace my next test on Tuesday."

Long-term goals are things that you would like to accomplish in your life. There are no time restraints. Just put down your goals and believe that they will happen. Example: "I will graduate college and find a job I love."

Now . . .

Take a piece of paper and write down the four components.

Take some time to think about each part and then jot down your responses for each of them.

Type out what you've written, print some copies, and keep them in places where you will review them daily. Feel free to add to the list at any time and replace the old copies.

Should you need some positive reinforcement, take some time to review the exercise:

Review the "Positive things in your life" section first. This will make you feel grateful for what you have, which will ultimately get you into a feel-good state.

Review all of your achievements. Going over all of your previous accomplishments will allow you to feel you are capable of achieving anything you set your mind to.

Review all of your short-term goals. Now that you are pumped from reviewing the positive things in your life and your accomplishments, you are in the right mindset to start reviewing your short-term goals.

Review your long-term goals. Thinking of the things you want to accomplish down the road and picturing your life five or ten years from now is a great way to end the exercise.

As always, be sure that you create your plan while experiencing a state of being of acceptance and see how quickly and unexpectedly you start achieving all of your goals!

Life Journey Plan

Positive things in my life

Achievements

Short-term goals

Long-term goals

100+ POSITIVE THINGS TO DO

When you are experiencing acceptance and you want to take an action that will expand that experience, try one of the following. This is a list of some fun, simple things to do that will not only expand your experience of happiness, but also expand the happiness of the person you share them with. I compiled this list with the help of my fiancée's younger sister Giavanna. Have fun with these!

1. Say thank you to someone.
2. Tell someone to have a nice day.
3. Congratulate someone.
4. Tell someone something sweet.
5. Let someone cut in front of you in line at a store.
6. Give a donation to an organization.
7. Help an elder cross the street.
8. Thank a professor for teaching.
9. Write someone a letter of encouragement.
10. Send someone a birthday card.
11. Let someone take your seat on the bus.
12. E-mail a friend a positive quote.
13. Send your parents flowers.
14. Write your partner a love letter.
15. Go nature walking.
16. Plant some trees where you feel they are needed.
17. Become a mentor.
18. Give gifts to underprivileged children during the holidays.
19. Read a book to a child.

20. Tell someone a joke.

21. Invite someone over for dinner.

22. Let someone borrow your favorite toy.

23. Bring a friend on vacation.

24. Buy a friend lunch.

25. Tell a family member you love him or her.

26. Be there for a friend on Valentine's Day.

27. Pick up trash on the sidewalk.

28. Convince a friend or family member not to smoke.

29. Give advice to a friend.

30. Help your parents or partner do the laundry.

31. Help a friend study.

32. Give someone a hug.

33. Bake someone a cake (or cupcakes).

34. Help a friend decorate his apartment.

35. Throw a surprise party.

36. Make someone chicken soup.

37. Let someone borrow a pen.

38. Congratulate a coworker on a raise or promotion.

39. Give a friend a ride.

40. Let someone walk under your umbrella.

41. Tell your boss he or she is doing a great job.

42. Organize a family fun night.

43. Have a slumber party with friends

44. Bring your partner to a special dinner.

45. Come up with a great idea at work.

46. Go visit your grandparents.

47. Make your parents breakfast in bed.

48. Tip a little extra next time you eat out.

49. Give a friend a piece of gum.

50. Let a coworker borrow a movie.

51. Watch a neighbor's child for free.

52. Volunteer your time at a soup kitchen.

53. Shovel your neighbor's driveway for free.

54. Give more candy at Halloween.

55. Apologize for something you did wrong.

56. Buy your friend tickets to a baseball game.

57. Cover your friend's movie ticket.

58. Coach a little league team.

59. Smile at someone you do not know.

60. Help a friend build something.

61. Adopt a dog.

62. Carve a pumpkin with a friend.

63. Create an Easter egg hunt for kids.

64. Take a dance class with a friend or family member.

65. Take up a hobby you have always wanted to do.

66. Help someone find a lost item.

67. Climb a mountain.

68. Travel the world.

69. Watch a neighbor's dog.

70. Let someone borrow your cell phone.

71. Help someone stranded on the highway.

72. Give the person who delivers your mail a holiday gift.

73. Spend some time outdoors on sunny days.

74. Be happy when it rains.

75. Tell someone something interesting.

76. Bring your dog to the park.

77. Wash your friend's car.

78. Buy lemonade at a kids' stand.

79. Fill your friend's gas tank.

80. Fix someone's bike.

81. Save a bug.

82. Be the first to initiate a conversation.

83. Set a goal and achieve it.

84. Adopt a child.

85. Help someone clean something that spilled.

86. Bring a friend or family member to work.

87. Buy your friend your favorite music CD.

88. Let a child win in a game.

89. Go visit a friend you have not seen.

90. Help a student with a homework assignment.

91. Go to a party with a friend.

92. Thank a firefighter for his or her work.

93. Bring flowers home for your partner.

94. Go to a senior citizen home for the day.

95. Change someone's tire.

96. Give someone a jump start.

97. Donate clothes to those in need.

98. Push a grocery cart back to the store.

99. Buy someone coffee.

100. Help someone fix his or her computer.

Here are ten more! Keep it going.

101. Let a friend use your home.

102. Take out the garbage for your parents.

103. Include a friend in on a secret.

104. Be the designated driver.

105. Become a volunteer firefighter.

106. Help a friend clean his or her pool.

107. Tie a friend's bow tie.

108. Give your partner a massage.

109. Donate a turkey during Thanksgiving.

110. Let a child help you with a project.

RESOURCES TO INSPIRE YOU

BOOKS

Excuse Me, Your Life Is Waiting: The Astonishing Power of Feelings, by Lynn Grabhorn

Excuse Me, Your Life Is Now: Mastering the Law of Attraction, by Doreen Banaszak

Blink: The Power of Thinking without Thinking, by Malcolm Gladwell

Body Ritual among the Nacirema, by Horace Mitchell Miner

Conversations with God, by Neale Donald Walsch

The Diving Bell and the Butterfly, by Jean-Dominique Bauby

Everyday Positive Thinking, by Louise L. Hay and Friends

The Four Agreements: A Practical Guide to Personal Freedom, by Miguel Ruiz

Happiness in a Box: 52 Instant Mood Boosters, by Karen Salmansohn and Frank Frisari

A New Earth: Awakening to Your Life's Purpose, by Eckhart Tolle

The Secret, by Rhonda Byrne

WEBSITES

Doreen Banaszak's website: www.excusemeyourlifeisnow.com

Sebastian Oddo's website: www.positivefeelingsrule.com

Karen Salmansohn's website: www.notsalmon.com

Lisa Fabbri's website: www.openflame.biz

Free Hugs Campaign: www.youtube.com

Music Therapy: www.musictherapy.org

Andrea Sun, Play for Prosperity and Wellbeing coach/speaker: www.ntpages.com.au/therapist/7130

Index

About the Authors

Doreen Banaszak is the author of *Excuse Me, Your Life Is Now.* Currently a teacher and life coach, she left a fifteen-year corporate career to create the life and business she really wanted. Through her teaching, writing, and coaching, she has been instrumental in helping people create the lives they really want, not the lives they think they should have. Doreen  offers one-on-one coaching as well as group presentations on mastering the Law of Attraction. Find out more on her website: www.excusemeyourlifeisnow.com.

Sebastian Oddo graduated from Manhattanville College with a BA in management and computer science. He is the founder of PositiveFeelingsRule.com, a website dedicated to helping young adults create and live positive lives. He currently lives in Westchester, New York, with his fiancée, Charly-Ann Melfi.

Hampton Roads Publishing Company

. . . for the evolving human spirit

HAMPTON ROADS PUBLISHING COMPANY publishes
books on a variety of subjects, including
spirituality, health, and other related topics.

For a copy of our latest trade catalog,
call toll-free, 800-766-8009, or send your name and address to:

HAMPTON ROADS PUBLISHING COMPANY, INC.
1125 STONEY RIDGE ROAD · CHARLOTTESVILLE, VA 22902
e-mail: hrpc@hrpub.com · www.hrpub.com